TIME

RELATIONSHIPS

MONEY

GOD

simple
life

ACTION PLAN

THOM S. RAINER & ART RAINER

LifeWay Press®
Nashville, Tennessee

Published by LifeWay Press®
© 2009 Thom S. Rainer and Art Rainer
Second printing 2011

ISBN 978-1-4158-6812-6
Item 005238065

Dewey decimal classification: 248.4
Subject headings: QUALITY OF LIFE \ STRESS MANAGEMENT \
LIFE SKILLS

Unless otherwise indicated, Scripture quotations are taken from
the Holman Christian Standard Bible®, copyright © 1999, 2000,
2002, 2003 by Holman Bible Publishers. Scripture quotations
marked NIV are from the Holy Bible, New International Version,
copyright © 1973, 1978, 1984 by International Bible Society.

To order additional copies of this resource, write to LifeWay Church
Resources Customer Service; One LifeWay Plaza; Nashville, TN
37234-0113; fax (615) 251-5933; phone toll free (800) 458-2772;
order online at *www.lifeway.com*; e-mail *orderentry@lifeway.com*;
or visit the LifeWay Christian Store serving you.

Printed in the United States of America

Leadership and Adult Publishing
LifeWay Church Resources
One LifeWay Plaza
Nashville, TN 37234-0175

CONTENTS

THE AUTHORS

Thom S. Rainer is the president and chief executive officer of LifeWay Christian Resources in Nashville, Tennessee. Prior to assuming this position in 2006, Thom was the dean of the Billy Graham School of Missions, Evangelism, and Church Growth at the Southern Baptist Theological Seminary, where he had served as a professor of evangelism and church growth.

Thom's books include *Simple Church*, *Breakout Churches*, *The Unchurched Next Door*, *High-Expectation Churches*, *Effective Evangelistic Churches*, and *Transformational Church* (forthcoming).

A native of Alabama, Thom holds a bachelor of science from the University of Alabama and a master of divinity and a doctor of philosophy from the Southern Baptist Theological Seminary.

Art Rainer serves as a staff member at First Baptist Church in West Palm Beach, Florida. He holds a master's degree in business administration from the University of Kentucky and is pursuing a doctorate in business administration.

Art also authored *Raising Dad* with his father.

The Simple Revolution

■ SESSION 1
Group Experience

1. Introduce yourself.
2. Share one way your life is not simple and one way you would like to simplify your life if possible.
3. Jesus said in John 10:10, "I have come that they may have life and have it in abundance." What do you think it takes to have the abundant life Jesus was talking about? How do complexity and busyness interfere with the abundant life?

Four Areas of Life

1. Show the DVD for session 1. Complete the viewer guide below.

The Simple Revolution

Four Steps Toward the Simple Life

_____
_____
_____
_____

Four Areas of Life

_____
_____
_____
_____

2. What statements in the video stood out as significant to you?
3. Identify the four areas of life on which this study will focus. Which area is the greatest source of complexity for you? Why?

Four Steps Toward the Simple Life

1. According to the authors, what steps will move you toward the simple life?
2. Identify some before-and-after phrases that express your goals for this study. One is provided as an example.

From _complexity_ to _____simplicity_____

From _____ to _____

From _____ to _____

From _____ to _____

From _____ to _____

From _____ to _____

From _____ to _____

From _____ to _____

3. Share your favorite phrase with the group. Use blank lines to jot down phrases that other group members share.
4. Share prayer concerns related to your need to simplify. Spend time praying silently that you will persevere and gain victory over the obstacles to a simpler life. Pray that your priorities will reflect God's will for your life.

Over the next six weeks you will read devotionals five days each week that will help you understand the four action steps and apply them to the four key areas of your life. You will also complete learning activities that will guide you to implement these steps in your life. You will establish goals for the four key areas of your life, and you will begin making changes to live with simplicity and intentionality.

Complete week 1 devotionals and activities before the next group session.

If you missed this session, go to www.lifeway.com/downloads
to download this or any other session of Simple Life.

WEEK 1

Introduction

Imagine a day like this.

You awake in the morning. You lie there a moment and thank God for a good night's rest and for the opportunities of a new day. Then you stop and think, *What day is it anyway? Thursday. Yes, it's Thursday.* You pray that you will honor God in all you do today, and you roll out of bed and head for the shower, trying to recall your to-do list for the day. At work you have meetings at 9:00 and 2:00. You have a birthday lunch that's been planned for more than a week. You'll have to stay focused to make any progress on your assignments today. Then the kids have a soccer game after school, and you have a stewardship-committee meeting after church tonight. It looks like dinner on the run. Catch-up with your spouse will be on the run with a cell phone again. You've just got to plan a date for the two of you soon.

You get home about 9:30, check on the kids, and say good night. You look through the mail; decide you are too tired to read the newspaper; and check your e-mail, voice mail, and text messages one last time for the day while you grab a peanut-butter-and-jelly sandwich to make up for the dinner you skipped. You fall asleep watching the evening news, get up, and collapse into bed.

Before you fall asleep, you thank God for the day. Then you remember everything you didn't get done today and what you need to do tomorrow. You recall that you had intended to take out the garbage tonight since tomorrow is pickup day. You fall asleep reminding yourself that taking out the garbage is your first priority in the morning.

No one wants garbage to be the day's first priority. How did life get to be this crazy and hectic? You long to slow down, to live with greater meaning and intentionality. You want the simple life.

simple life

Like most people today, you are busy; there's no question about that. But the more you think about it, the more you wonder where your life is going. Where is all the busyness taking you? On your most recent significant birthday ending in a zero, you began to add up the hours and the days and paused to consider whether you were spending them the way you would if you had a choice.

Do you have a choice? Many people are considering their choices in how they are living their hours and their days. And they are choosing to simplify their lives. Instead of letting other people, events, and obligations determine their priorities, they are reevaluating their lives, making some hard decisions, and setting a new course, a new direction in life. So many are taking these steps that you could say there's a simple revolution going on.

If you feel that your life is out of control, that you are not spending your limited time and money on the things that are most important to you, that circumstances you have allowed to take over your life are hurting your relationships with people and with God, then perhaps you too want to become a revolutionary.

What has been the worst part of your day?

Your week?

Stressed-out is not how God intends for us to live. Read what Jesus said in the Sermon on the Mount about worrying:

This is why I tell you: Don't worry about your life, what you will eat or what you will drink; or about your body, what you will wear. Isn't life more than food and the body more than clothing? Look at the birds of the sky: they don't sow or reap or gather into barns, yet your heavenly Father feeds them. Aren't you worth more than they? Can any of you add a single cubit to his height by worrying? And why do you worry about clothes? Learn how the wildflowers of the field grow: they don't labor or spin thread. Yet I tell you that not even Solomon in all his splendor was adorned like one of these! If that's how God clothes the grass of the field, which is here today and thrown into the furnace tomorrow, won't He do much more for you—you of little faith? So don't worry, saying, "What will we eat?" or "What will we drink?" or "What will we wear?" For the idolaters eagerly seek all these things, and your heavenly Father knows that you need them. But seek first the kingdom of God and His righteousness, and all these things will be provided for you. Therefore don't worry about tomorrow, because tomorrow will worry about itself. Each day has enough trouble of its own (Matt. 6:25-34).

What are the greatest sources of worry and stress in your life at present?

How do Jesus' words about worrying apply to your situation?

God said to Jeremiah, "I know the plans I have for you … plans for your welfare, not for disaster, to give you a future and a hope" (Jer. 29:11). Are you so busy that you might be missing out on God's plans for you both now and in the future?

The process outlined in this workbook will help you examine four significant areas of your life:

1. Time
2. Relationships
3. Money
4. God

Two of these areas deal with your limited resources—time and money. And two deal with relationships with other people—spouse, children, other family members, friends, coworkers—and with God.

Are you satisfied with the way you spend your time and your money? ☐ Yes ☐ No

Are you satisfied with your relationships with your family—spouse, children, other family members, friends, coworkers—and with God? ☐ Yes ☐ No

Would you make some changes if someone outlined a process to help you make the changes you desire? ☐ Yes ☐ No

You may find that you are right where you want to be and where you believe God wants you to be in these four areas of your life. You may discover that you want to make small changes in your life in one or two areas. Or you may find that at least one area of your life needs a bigger shift.

When you make adjustments in one area, you affect the others. For example, if you decide to save more money for retirement, you'll have to cut back on something else. If you decide to cut back on entertainment, it may mean your kids won't have the newest electronic game system, and you might have to delay the purchase of the digital camera you wanted for your next vacation. And your vacation might also be delayed or shortened! How will that affect your relationships with family members?

You may decide to spend more time in daily devotionals. You'd like to do that first thing in the morning. Can you do that and help get the kids off to school? Can you do that and continue to carpool? This simple shift to work on your relationship with God will impact your time and your relationships with others.

Can you think of a change that would make your life better, simpler, or more purposeful? How? Write your thoughts.

As you examine your time, relationships, money, and God, you'll follow a four-step process:

1. Clarity
2. Movement
3. Alignment
4. Focus

Taking these actions can help you move from chaos to control, from meaningless busyness to purpose and fulfillment. Is it simple? Yes. Easy? No. You'll find that following the four-step process in each area of your life (time, relationships, money, and God) is doable. It will make a huge difference in your life. But it won't always be easy. Saying yes to redirecting your life so that you can maximize your priorities means saying no to some time-stealing, money-guzzling activities and relationships. Choosing the simple life means eliminating some things in life that you may enjoy in order to elevate those things that are most important.

Making the tough choices will be worth the effort, however, in order to join the simple revolution, to find the simple life you desire. But before you begin the journey to a simple life, let's look at the revolution that's taking place all around us. Then we'll take a closer look at the four areas of your life and the process for change.

simple life

If you are looking for the simple life, you are not alone. We have had the incredible opportunity to listen to more than one thousand people across America. They come from every geographic area, a diversity of races and ethnic groups, and across the age spectrum. They are nearly equally divided between genders.

Their stories are different; but at the same time, they have similar themes. Life is stressful. Life is busy. Not enough time for the things that really matter. And most of the time, they tell us they feel financial stress as well.

The answer? Americans are rediscovering simple. At least they are aware that they need to rediscover simple. People are hungry for simple because the world has become much more complex. The technology revolution has really become an information revolution. We have access to more information, more products, more research, and more ideas than at any point in history. But the information revolution and the material wealth of Americans have made life for many people much more complex.

Eric Geiger and I (Thom) wrote *Simple Church* a few years ago. We were amazed at the response. Church leaders wanted simple. Church members wanted simple. In the midst of the harried world of complexity and uncontrollably complex lives, people want to find simple for their lives. They long for it, seek it, pay for it, and even dream of it.

The simple-life revolution has begun. And we're finding it not only in churches but also in individuals. Our surveys show that people are desperately seeking the simple life.

simple**life** STATISTICS ■

41 *questions*
1,077 *respondents*
57% *female*
43% *male*
80% *Christians*

As in all things we can turn to Jesus as our example and our inspiration. He didn't have to contend with e-mail, cell phones, tweets, or pages—and maybe we can learn from that. We are amazed at the simplicity of His earthly life. Despite the demands of the entire world on His life and time, He spent time with His friends. He loved little children. He gave attention to those in need. He spent time with His Father. But He was also a revolutionary; He turned the world upside down.

In the Sermon on the Mount (Matt. 5), Jesus said those who are blessed are the poor, the hungry, those who are mourning, and those who are persecuted. He said that looking at a woman with lust in your heart is the same as committing adultery. He said to turn the other cheek and to love your enemies.

Think about qualities you most admire in Jesus as He lived His life on earth. List them here.

Review your list and circle one or two characteristics of Jesus that you wish were more evident in your life.

How would simplifying your life help you live with the priorities Jesus had while on earth?

simple life

When we concluded our study of 1,077 individuals, we learned that they needed simple in four areas.

1. **Time.** This theme was present in all of the areas, but it was a theme unto itself as well. Those surveyed wanted simple so that they could find time for the areas of their lives that really mattered.
2. **Relationships.** Many respondents struggled with balance in relationships. The simple life for them meant more opportunities for closer relationships.
3. **Money.** Financial strains were pervasive with many in this study. They longed for a simple life free of past-due bills, limited income, deficient savings, and increasing debt.
4. **God.** These people, above all, saw a big void in their relationship with God. Aware of the irony that they were too busy for God, they longed for a simpler life to get closer to Him.

We know we can't replicate all Jesus did. But we can pattern our lives after Him. He kept His focus on what really mattered and managed His time accordingly. And so should we.

Read the following Scripture passages and identify ways Jesus spent His time.

Matthew 4:23:

Matthew 12:1:

John 7:33:

Read the following Scripture passages and record ways Jesus placed priority on relationships.

Matthew 19:13-14:

Mark 6:31:

John 3:22:

John 11:5:

Read the following Scripture passages and describe Jesus' attitude toward money.

Matthew 6:24:

Matthew 21:12:

Matthew 26:6-10:

Mark 12:41-44:

Read the following Scripture passages and identify ways Jesus placed priority on His relationship with His Father.

Matthew 6:6:

Matthew 14:23:

Matthew 19:29:

Matthew 26:36:

Mark 1:35:

Mark 6:46:

Look through the verses again. They are grouped under the categories of time, relationships, money, and God. As you read them again, write in the margin another area to which the verse might apply.

From these verses, what lesson from Jesus' dealings with time, relationships, money, and God can you apply in your own life?

simple life

As we examine the four key areas of your life and outline a process for change, we will use the four words Thom and Eric introduced in *Simple Church*. They are *clarity*, *movement*, *alignment*, and *focus*. These words are important, so let's clarify what they mean.

■ Clarity

Clarity means you know where you are going. Before you move closer to the simple life, you need a blueprint of where you are going. You need clarity.

Each week we will challenge you to develop a clear plan toward the simple life:

- How do you plan to spend time on the things that really matter in life?
- What is your plan for developing healthier relationships?
- How do you plan to get your finances in order?
- What is your plan for getting closer to God?

You probably noticed the redundancy of the word *plan*. Clarity means that you have a plan and that the plan clearly states where you want to go. We will even encourage you to write your own mission statement for each of the four areas. But don't leave that mission statement as an inactive file in your computer. Let it be the blueprint toward the simple life.

We all know we need more clarity in these four areas, but most of the time we don't make a plan. Let us share with you some of the heartfelt cries of those we surveyed. See if you can hear the clarity they need to move toward the simple life:

- "I want to be able to spend more time with my child instead of working all the time and having him go to day care."
- "I would just love for the kids to get along and quit fighting so that we could have some peace in the house."
- "I spend too much time taking everyone where they need to be when they need to be there."
- "I want a job that would satisfy all of our financial needs without taking time away from our family time."
- "We are constantly on the go due to our children's sporting events. Whether it's for practice, scrimmages, or games of multiple sports, we are gone from home almost every night of the week."
- "I wish we could pay off all our debt. It would take a lot of stress off at home and let us spend more time together."
- "We all need to be on the same page spiritually. Our relationship with God is an afterthought in our family."

We will begin each week's study by focusing on clarity. Simply stated, we will help you see the path you need to travel. Paul wrote about achieving God's goals for his life:

Not that I have already reached the goal or am already fully mature, but I make every effort to take hold of it because I also have been taken hold of by Christ Jesus. Brothers, I do not consider myself to have taken hold of it. But one thing I do: forgetting what is behind and reaching forward to what is ahead,I pursue as my goal the prize promised by God's heavenly call in Christ Jesus. Therefore, all who are mature should think this way. And if you think differently about anything, God will reveal this to you also (Phil. 3:12-15).

Paul also wrote, "When I was a child, I spoke like a child, I thought like a child, I reasoned like a child. When I because a man, I put aside childish things. For now we see indistinctly, as in a mirror, but then face to face. Now I know in part, but then I will know fully, as I am fully known" (1 Cor. 13:11-12). Maturity is God's desire for us. If we ask Him, He will help us clearly see the changes we need to make.

Write your own definition of *clarity* and describe how this step can help you move toward a simple life.

■ Movement

Congestion is rarely a good thing. The word can take on different meanings, but few if any of them are good. *Congestion* means *to be blocked up* or *to be too full of something*. Whether referring to sinuses or highways, congestion is bad.

Congestion in life means you aren't moving toward the goal. To make progress, you need to identify and remove the obstacles. I (Thom) was 40 pounds overweight for four years. Why? Because I had no movement toward my goal. Wishing and hoping didn't get the job done. Then one day I visited my youngest son, Jess, to find him slimmer and healthier than ever. He inspired me. I made commitments to eat better and exercise more. I removed the congestion. I had movement toward my goal. Today I am 40 pounds lighter and feeling great.

In each of the four areas of time, relationships, money, and God, we will look at movement—how we can remove the congestion or obstacles to get where we need to go. Movement involves two elements.

1. Movement is intentional. We are sometimes asked how we write a book. It's not rocket science. We are just intentional. We purposefully act on our plan.

After you have decided that you will make better use of your time, you act on it. You are intentional. The same is true for healthy relationships. And the same is true for financial health. You are intentional. After you have decided that you want to get closer to God, you act on it. You are intentional.

2. Movement is incremental. You don't try to conquer the world in a day. You take short-term steps. You have the clarity of where you want to go, but you don't try to arrive at your destination all at once.

For example, if you want to be healthier, you may start with a mild exercise program, take a multivitamin, or start eating healthier foods. You have literally dozens of choices, but you take only one or a few steps. If you try to do everything at once, you will become frustrated and give up.

That's the way it is with the simple life. Movement requires taking incremental steps so that you won't give up.

Write your own definition of *movement* and describe how this step can help you move toward a simple life.

■ Alignment

As we delve into the tough issues of moving toward the simple life, we need to look at areas where we go wrong, where our lives are out of line with our goals. Most of the time, it takes only one small misstep to evolve into a major problem. Most people don't have debt problems overnight. Most Christians don't stop attending church suddenly. Most relationships don't fail over one incident. Most people don't become workaholics in one day. Instead, their lives get out of alignment. It begins small. But it doesn't remain small. You can't reach your goals if your daily habits and activities don't line up with your stated objectives. We will help you identify ways to make sure your personal choices and actions align with the goals you have set for your life

Write your own definition of *alignment* and describe how this step can help you move toward a simple life.

Focus

After you clearly state where you want to go (clarity), begin making incremental steps in the right direction (movement), and match your daily life to your stated goals (alignment), you are ready to eliminate some good stuff. Yep, you read right. You eliminate some good stuff.

You see, it is one thing to get those bad habits and problems out of the way. But it is another thing to stop doing some good things. We call this last phase *focus*.

Many problems we heard in this study were not always the result of doing bad things. As we looked at the lives of those who graciously participated in the study, we saw many good intentions. In fact, we saw too many good intentions. We saw families take on activity after activity. We saw work lives that became workaholism. We saw the good become the bad because there was just too much of the good.

The simple life demands that we eliminate some things. It means we have to make some tough decisions. In fact, focus may very well be the toughest step toward the simple life. But it is absolutely necessary.

Write your own definition of *focus* and describe how this step can help you move toward a simple life.

Clarity. Movement. Alignment. Focus. These four strategies will bring you closer to the simple life.

simple life

A mission statement is a goal that defines the decisions and actions of an individual or organization, based on values and priorities. For example, your church may have a mission statement that states its God-given purpose in the community, state, nation, and world. Many church mission statements are based on the Great Commission in Matthew 28:19-20 or Acts 1:8. Your business may have a mission statement that defines the company's purpose. Perhaps you have a personal mission statement, a purpose you have discerned that God has uniquely gifted and commissioned you to do.

From the goals defined in these mission statements, decisions are made about the ways valuable resources like time and money will be spent. Mission statements not only help people, churches, businesses, and other organizations determine what they will do; they also help them decide what they will not do. In order to do well what they have stated they will do, the person, business, church, or other organization must eliminate or choose not to do other things—even good things— to excel at the task outlined in the mission statement.

If your church has a mission statement, record it here.

Identify some of your church's ministries that directly flow from that mission statement.

When you write a mission statement that defines your life purpose, you should consider what you like to do; your personality; your unique combination of gifts, talents, abilities, interests, strengths, and weaknesses; and what you believe God has called you to do. Unless God specifically directed otherwise, a good mission statement for introverts probably would not focus on a purpose that continually forced them to initiate contacts or to be public speakers. Someone who is 5'6" tall might not want a mission statement to become a player for the NBA.

> List some of your gifts, talents, abilities, interests, strengths, and weaknesses.

Your gifts and abilities will have a direct effect on your mission statements. For example, maybe you want to grow in your relationship with God, but you've struggled all your life with having a daily quiet time. You have difficulty sitting still, staying focused, and reading or remaining silent for long periods of time. You may not want to set a goal of getting up at 4:30 each morning to pray for an hour. But you may want to set a goal (write a mission statement) of listening to the Bible on a CD every day for 40 days. Or you may want to write a mission statement like this:

> *As I will walk for 30 minutes three days a week, I will pray and listen to what God has to say.*

Your mission statement should be like your favorite clothes. It should fit well and be comfortable. Jesus said, "My yoke is easy and My burden is light" (Matt. 11:30). He wasn't saying to rest, take it easy, and enjoy life. He was saying that when you do His work, if you obey Him and stay the course, like the oxen in the harness pulling the plow, the yoke will fit well. Obeying Christ in what He is calling you to do is the foundation of any mission statement.

> Read Jonah 1. How did God discipline Jonah when he turned from what God wanted him to do?

A mission statement is important because it establishes clarity for your goals, which in turn guide your decisions and actions toward the simple life. In this study you will be asked to write not just one mission statement that applies to your whole life but four mission statements to identify your goals in the areas of time, relationships, money, and God. Your mission statements will be yours alone. You can choose to share them so that someone can hold you accountable, or you can keep them private, letting your statements guide your decisions about your resources (time and money) and your relationships (people and God).

To be valuable, a mission statement must be specific. It must state exactly what you intend to do to reach your goal. It must also be measurable; it must state how you will accomplish something and must include a completion date. For example, you may write this goal for your relationship with your parents:

Because I love my parents, I will make my relationship with them a priority.

That's a worthwhile goal, but it lacks specificity. A better mission statement might be:

Because I love my parents, I will call them at least twice a week, and I will visit them at least once a month.

This statement tells exactly how and when you will do something.

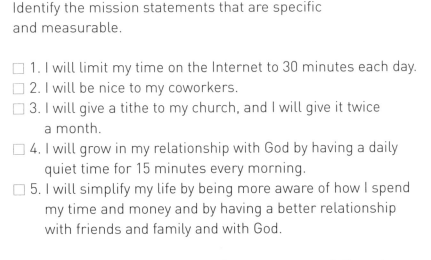

Identify the mission statements that are specific
and measurable.

☐ 1. I will limit my time on the Internet to 30 minutes each day.
☐ 2. I will be nice to my coworkers.
☐ 3. I will give a tithe to my church, and I will give it twice
a month.
☐ 4. I will grow in my relationship with God by having a daily
quiet time for 15 minutes every morning.
☐ 5. I will simplify my life by being more aware of how I spend
my time and money and by having a better relationship
with friends and family and with God.

If you chose 1, 3, 4, you are correct. These statements define what you will do and when you will do it.

The remaining five weeks in this study will guide you to understand and engage with the four areas of time, relationships, money, and God and will help you put together a holistic plan for your life at the end of the process. By the end of the study, you will have completed 30 devotionals that help you understand the four areas of life and the strategic steps of clarity, movement, alignment, and focus. Complete each suggested activity as an action plan that challenges you to move toward the simple life.

This study is not a quick-fix solution to get your life in order. It's a beginning. It's an action plan for the simple life. To that end we have prayed for you. We don't know you by name, but we know that the God to whom we pray knows everything about you. And by His power you can see despair become hope and confusion become simple.

Join us for the journey.

Join us for the victory.

Welcome to the simple life.

How to Make Your Time Really Count

SESSION 2
Group Experience

1. In the left column identify things that make your life busy, complex, frustrating, or out of control. In the right column write descriptions of an ideal, simple, purposeful life.

Out of Control   **Simple**

_____   _____

_____   _____

_____   _____

_____   _____

2. Label each item in the out-of-control column as related to either time, relationships, money, or God.
3. Share what you have written with other group members.
4. Discuss whether these four areas represent most of your life's frustrations. Why or why not?

Four Steps Toward the Simple Life

Discuss how each strategy will help move you toward the simple life.

1. Clarity   3. Alignment
2. Movement   4. Focus

A Life of Purpose

1. Turn to week 1, day 3, pages 15–17. Discuss the way Jesus lived and what He taught in regard to time, relationships, money, and God.
2. In what ways could you apply Jesus' life and teachings regarding time, relationships, money, and God to your life?

Mission Statements

1. Turn to week 1, day 5, page 23, and review the description of *mission statement*. Discuss its purpose.
2. What does it mean for a mission statement to be specific and measurable?
3. One component of this study will be to write a mission statement for each of the four life areas: time, relationships, money, and God. Review and evaluate the mission statements in the activity on page 26, identifying reasons some are better examples than others.

A Matter of Time

1. Show the DVD for session 2. Complete the viewer guide below.

How to Make Your Time Really Count

_____ percent of people participating in the simple-life survey indicated they will have health problems if they continue at their current pace.

Is the life you are living the life you were _____ to live?

2. Discuss Evelyn's story. In what ways can you relate to her?
3. Share prayer concerns related to your struggles with time, relationships, money, or God. Take turns praying that God will use this study to bring your lives into alignment with His purposes.

Complete week 2 devotionals and activities before the next group session.

If you missed this session, go to www.lifeway.com/downloads to download this or any other session of Simple Life.

simple
life

Evelyn sat on the other side of the desk and let out a deep sigh. "Jared and I are completely overwhelmed."

Evelyn, 34, and Jared had three kids. Evelyn had recently taken a new job with the city's newspaper. "Every day we are swamped. From the time we try to get our kids ready for school until the time they finally fall asleep, life is nonstop. Our youngest just started his first year of T-ball, so now we have three children in three separate leagues. It's a logistical nightmare. I don't even want to think about when the baseball season starts overlapping with soccer. And, of course, it's not just the kids. Jared and I are really dedicated to our careers."

Evelyn had always tried to put a positive spin on their busy lives. The kids were developing and getting opportunities. Their own careers were progressing. But these good things had come at a cost. They were losing control.

"Jared and I don't really spend much time with our children. And I miss the times when Jared and I would go out together, just the two of us. I miss dates. I couldn't tell you the last time we did something like that together."

Evelyn looked at her watch. "I've got to go. I have to pick up my oldest child from practice. Jared should be on his way to pick up the youngest." And with a half-smile and a head nod, she was gone.

Can you relate to Evelyn? Our culture is obsessed with time; yet we never have enough. This week we will look at time from God's perspective and set goals for the way we use our time. Then we will make sure our actions match our priorities so that we use our time for the important things in life instead of allowing time to control us.

Clarity
■ Day 1 It's About Time

■ Humans at Risk

Our culture places a very high value on time. We spend massive amounts of money developing new ways to increase the efficiency of our moments on earth. With each passing day, our culture becomes more and more proficient in ways to maximize time. Because of time-saving technology, we are able to do more, learn more, and experience more in a lifetime than any generations that preceded us.

And this is good. God created us with intellects to explore His world and to do great things with it. But we have a problem. Our obsession with time has become unhealthy. It has permeated areas of our lives it should have never entered.

In what ways can you relate to Evelyn's story on page 30?

☐ Rushing with kids' activities
☐ Demanding careers
☐ No time for spouse or other important relationships
☐ Other:

How did you get in this time crunch?

☐ By adding things I thought would benefit me and my family
☐ Pressure to achieve in my career
☐ Social pressure to be involved in activities
☐ Pressure to be involved in church activities
☐ Other:

Even if we started with good intentions, by adding on more and more, our lives quickly get out of control.

Busyness has consumed us.

In our research we were amazed to see that approximately 44 percent of respondents agreed that if their daily lives continued at the current pace, they would probably have health problems. That number is alarming. The stress of a go-go-go lifestyle has been linked to a number of health problems.

What, if any, health problems are you experiencing?

☐ Heart disease   ☐ Obesity   ☐ Memory problems
☐ Stress   ☐ Depression   ☐ Fatigue
☐ Irritability   ☐ Sleep disorder
☐ Anxiety   ☐ High blood pressure
☐ Other: _____

Our obsession with time has come at a high cost. We are literally putting our lives at risk for the pursuit of personal gain.

Of course, it is not just our physical health that is suffering. Our families are also impacted by this problem. Spouses don't have time for each other. Our children are also caught up in a whirlwind of activities, from soccer to ballet to French club. And we are all too busy for God, the giver of time.

simplelife   STATISTICS ■

44% *feel they will have health problems if their daily lives continue at the current pace.*
57% *rarely go on dates with their spouses.*
84% *need to spend more time with their spouses.*

▪ Made for Eternity

Christians are supposed to look at time differently. This life is literally a blip on the eternal time line. But because we live in a world in which time exists, we understandably struggle to wrap our minds around the infinite. But we still know it's there, waiting on us.

Read Ecclesiastes 3:11.

"[God] has made everything appropriate in its time. He has also put eternity in their hearts, but man cannot discover the work God has done from beginning to end" (Eccl. 3:11).

Why is it so difficult for us to live with eternity in mind?

God created us for eternity; yet while still time-bound, we can't fully grasp that eternal perspective. If we could somehow fully grasp the concept of never-ending, then our time on this planet would certainly be different. But we can't. We find it difficult to move beyond the day, much less the eternal. Consequently, we make choices based on the only time span that seems important—the blip.

Read Psalm 90, a psalm written by Moses. How did Moses describe God's view of time (see v. 4)?

How did Moses describe humans' view of time (v. 10)?

What did Moses conclude about the way we should use our time on earth (v. 12)?

Somehow we know our time, no matter how brief it may be, is highly important. We know our life and what we do with it matter. We know God, who set this whole thing in motion with a quick spin of the globe, passionately watches over this place dubbed Earth. He cares what happens to me and to you. He cares about what we do with our days and our moments He has given us.

However, God doesn't want us to fret about today or tomorrow (see Matt. 6:34). Although this life will allow us to make an impact for all eternity, good or bad, it's only the starting point.

So here we are, temporarily fixed by time. We built our lives trying to accomplish much and trying to help our family succeed, but this grand structure of a life we envisioned now suddenly seems more like a prison. We are stressed and overwhelmed, and we want out.

By constantly remaining busy, we are hurting ourselves and others. How long can this continue? How fast are we able to go until something falls apart? What will be the breaking point? The frantic way we do life cannot be sustained.

Of course, you already know this. You understand that you are at risk. You see that the ability to "have time" is dwindling in your life. The day has become way too full. Time has become a luxury to you.

And you don't want it that way. You want something different.

Something more.

And yet something less.

The simple life.

Clarity

■ **Day 2** Being Clear with Our Priorities

■ Figuring Out Time

Decisions about the wise use of time begin with identifying your priorities in life. Ideally, the way you use time should reflect what you value most in life. Unfortunately, this is not always the case.

One of the most powerful stories in the Bible about the relationship between priorities and time is found in Luke 10:38-42. The story involves two sisters, Mary and Martha. Lazarus, Jesus' friend whom He would later raise from the dead, was their brother. Both sisters loved Jesus, but each demonstrated her love in her own way.

Read Luke 10:38-42. What was Martha doing during Jesus' visit?

What was Mary doing?

Which sister did Jesus commend and why?

Martha had busied herself so much that she missed what was most important. Her desires were good, but the outcome fell short. While she was frenetically preparing for the feast of men, she was missing a feast for the heart.

Martha's more became less.

Mary's less became more.

Are you more like Mary or Martha? In what ways?

■ Moving Toward Clarity

Today you will follow a process to identify your priorities and then write a mission statement for your use of time.

Let's start with a real-life example. Remember Evelyn? You read her story on page 30. She and her husband were having trouble balancing their careers and their family life. We asked Evelyn to sit down and record her activities in a typical day. They included her children's sports, her and Jared's jobs, church activities, exercise, and so on.

Evelyn then reflected on what she thought her priorities should be in life. She wrote those down and ranked them:

1. God   2. Family   3. Health

Then Evelyn compared her list of priorities to the way she was using her time each day. The two lists were not the same. Her day told a different story than her heart. Like many of us, Evelyn realized that the life she was living was causing dissatisfaction in her heart. So she decided she needed to make some modifications. She wrote this statement of change in regard to the way she used her time:

In order to make the day reflect my priorities, I will work only a maximum of two hours overtime a week, spend 30 minutes daily reading the Bible and praying, allow my children to play only two sports a year, and have one date with my husband each week.

Let's go through the same process Evelyn followed to identify your priorities, to evaluate your use of time, and to write a mission statement that reflects your goals for change.

First write what you consider to be the priorities in your life— what you consider to be most important.

Your priorities might look something like this:
1. God   2. Family   3. Health   4. Friends   5. Work

Take a few minutes to record your activities during a typical 24-hour day, whether you work inside or outside the home. Account for all 24 hours in 30-minute increments, including sleeping and eating. For example, if you work for four consecutive hours, record the time you worked (8:00 to 12:00), the number of hours worked (4), and the activity (work).

Time	Hours/Minutes	Activity

What does your time log reveal about your priorities in life? How are you spending most of your time? What defines your day?

Now compare your daily activities with the list of priorities you recorded on page 36. How does your typical day reflect or neglect your stated priorities?

If you are like most people, your priorities aren't where you desire them to be. Your heart yearns for your time log to read differently. And that's good. We were created to live differently. That yearning is your desire to live your life as you were meant to live it, to have your life reflect its proper priorities.

Next you will write a mission statement that reflects your desire to align your use of time with your priorities in life. A good mission statement has the following characteristics.

- Your mission statement should reflect your life priorities.
- Your mission statement must be clear and concise.
- Your mission statement should convey an intention to put it into action.
- Your mission statement should be realistic and achievable.

With your priorities and the previous guidelines in mind, write a mission statement for your use of time.

The simple life means rearranging your daily life in a way that reflects the priorities of your heart. Tomorrow you will identify barriers you need to eliminate to achieve your goals for using your time.

Movement

There will be barriers that prevent you from living out your mission statement, but don't throw in the towel early. You should expect hindrances in your path. Hindrances brought you to this point. The accumulation of those hindrances caused you to want something different for yourself, to pursue a different way of doing life.

When you decide to take the next step, to move beyond staring at your mission statement and actually put it into action, you need to clear out any obstructions that might encumber your movement to a simple life.

> Review the mission statement you wrote on page 38. Does it say all you want it to say? If you knew you didn't have much time to live, would this statement move you to where you want to be?

Let's examine some of the obstacles that threaten to keep us from fulfilling our mission for our use of time.

■ Choices

Our lives are the culmination of our choices. For most of us, it is by choice that we were put into a time crunch, and it will be by choice that we get out of it. There's not a magic wand we can wave to eliminate our hectic day. We have to be willing to come face-to-face with whatever stands in the way of our mission statement and to decide to eliminate it.

We hope your life has been characterized by great decisions. But we also know that, like us, you have probably made some choices that weren't the best, some from which you are now suffering. That's fine. We all make mistakes. They are some of life's greatest teachers.

> Identify a choice you made that is now interfering with your priorities in life.
>
> ☐ Working too much
> ☐ Overly committed to your social life
> ☐ Meeting your kids' every demand
> ☐ Other:

One of the great things about choice is that by choice you can reverse a previous decision. The course of your day hinges on your decisions. With courage and wisdom you can make decisions that eliminate your time burdens.

simplelife   STATISTICS ■

68% *would change their day if they could.*

■ Self-Absorption

Recall the story of Martha, Mary, and Jesus. Wanting to be a good host, Martha fretted over the appearance of her house and meal preparation for her guests. But what might not seem like a bad characteristic quickly became a hindrance: she failed to see what she really needed. Martha busied herself so that she could appear as she wanted to be seen, not as Jesus wanted to see her.

In two sentences Martha revealed that her work was about more than just meeting the needs of her guests but actually focused on herself: "Lord, don't You care that my sister has left me to serve alone? Tell her to give me a hand!" (Luke 10:40). It had become all about her.

Self-absorption hinders our moving into a simple life. We are convinced that this life is about us and our appearance. Much of our time is spent trying to create an image that says, "I have it all together." From our looks, to our careers, to our lifestyle, to our children, we want to be the whole package. And our time becomes filled with things that help us reach that elusive goal.

List ways you spend your time that are designed to enhance your image or reputation.

Don't you hate looking at the motivations for your actions and decisions? When we dig down deep and ask ourselves probing questions about the time we spend on our activities, the results can get ugly. We begin to realize that we treat ourselves as the center of our universe. Asking ourselves, "Why?" and truthfully answering that question helps us uncover the underlying purpose behind many of our actions.

- Why do I work so many hours?
- Why are my children involved in so many activities?
- Why do I spend so much time at the gym?
- Why am I on so many councils?
- Why do I volunteer so much?

Select a question in the previous list that applies to you and answer it honestly.

Our drive to become the perfect human with the perfect family and the perfect career creates self-imposed barriers that limit us from achieving the simple life. We have to figure out what is truly necessary and what is just an outflow of our ego. Those who are able to keep their egos in check will find it easier to achieve a simple life.

■ Dealing with the Past, Fretting About the Future, and Forgetting the Present

It may be that we have erected barriers to achieving simplicity to protect ourselves from our own insecurities. Many of us fill our days with time-consuming activities so that we don't have to face who we really are.

Mark, for example, is a highly successful executive, but that isn't enough. You see, Mark grew up with a hypercritical father. Nothing was ever good enough. His dad never really made it past middle management, and that bothered him. Mark's dad often took out his frustration and personal disappointment on Mark. Mark never heard his dad say, "I'm proud of you, Son." Mark's dad didn't find joy in his own accomplishments, so he resented Mark's successes. Mark did everything to try and win his dad's approval, to the point of becoming a workaholic.

But the approval never came.

Mark's dad passed away last year. Now Mark is still trying to prove himself to a father who is gone. He just wants to be good enough.

Is it wrong for us to be concerned with the future and to reflect on the past? Absolutely not. The past and the future are important, but their importance has limits. When we become overly concerned about the future, we concern ourselves with the unknown. When we try to overcompensate for the past, we try to break away from something that can't be changed. Those who do not find some type of compromise in their schedules will create obstacles to a simple life. They will fill their days with too much activity, trying to achieve the unachievable.

Identify anything in your past that motivates your use of time today.

Identify any fear about the future that motivates your use of time today.

Don't let the concerns of the past or future swallow up your time. Find perspective and give appropriate attention to them. Remove what may hinder a simple life. Move forward in the present.

Review your mission statement on page 38. Remember, it must be an action plan. It must reflect intentional movement. Look at where you are now in the use of your time and where you want to be. What barriers prevent you from simplifying your life? Check any that apply and note others below.

☐ Choices
☐ Self-consuming congestion
☐ Regret over the past
☐ Fear about the future
☐ Other:

Does your mission statement address some of those barriers, either implicitly or explicitly? In what ways?

◼ Letting Go

You've identified some areas in your life that may be impeding the movement of simplifying your time. You know you need to remove some things from your life but may be unsure which ones to focus on. Remember, your mission statement is your guide through this journey. Select just a few barriers to start with. Choose one that will be easy and one that might be a little challenging. Don't become overwhelmed with deconstructing the day you used to experience. Allow time to adjust as you remove each obstruction.

When you adjust, it's time to start looking for other obstructions that are preventing movement during your day. Continue to get rid of these until you are free of all that inhibits you from realizing your goals. You will gradually move closer to the simple life.

Toward the end of Deuteronomy, the leadership baton passed for the Hebrew nation. Moses had led the Israelites out of Egypt, crossed the Red Sea, followed a fiery cloud, and presented the Ten Commandments to the nation. Next up was Joshua, who had a deep faith that God would deliver the land to the Israelites as promised.

Read Moses' charge to Joshua in Deuteronomy 31:7-8:

"Moses then summoned Joshua and said to him in the sight of all Israel, 'Be strong and courageous, for you will go with this people into the land the LORD swore to give to their fathers. You will enable them to take possession of it. The LORD is the One who will go before you. He will be with you; He will not leave you or forsake you. Do not be afraid or discouraged' " (Deut. 31:7-8).

What would be Joshua's source of strength and courage?

☐ Joshua's physical endurance
☐ God's presence
☐ The Hebrew army

Moses promised Joshua and the nation that God would go before them. Because they could rely on Him, they didn't need to be afraid. As you develop clarity for your time, realize that you have a God who goes with you. He wants the very best for you and wants to see you succeed in making this part of your life simpler. Time was never meant to be a burden but a blessing. Each breath we are given is a gift from God. A reliance on Him is essential to moving you toward a simple life.

Removing or minimizing barriers isn't easy. Pray that God will give you wisdom to know which barriers to address and the strength to move toward their elimination.

Alignment

Alignment is structuring our life's activities and priorities so that we can accomplish our mission statement for the simple life. It is lining up our schedule so that it runs parallel to our heart's yearning.

This week we have discussed ways we can simplify our time. We have already eliminated activities that were not part of our declared priorities. Our next step will be figuring out how we can align our remaining daily activities so that they move us toward the realization of our mission statement. Alignment takes dedication; it takes sacrifice. But it is necessary for the simple life.

simple life   STATISTICS ■

69% *need to change how they use their time each day.*
40% *of born-again Christians regularly pray with their children.*
35% *of married Christians regularly pray with their spouses.*
30% *of married Christians read the Bible together at least once a week.*

■ Time for an Honest Assessment

When Martha questioned Jesus about Mary's perceived irresponsibility, He answered, "Martha, Martha, you are worried and upset about many things, but one thing is necessary. Mary has made the right choice, and it will not be taken away from her" (Luke 10:41-42).

Describe the alignment Jesus was asking Martha to make.

Jesus told Martha that, though she had many concerns, they were not correct concerns. For that moment her heart and mind were in the wrong place. We don't know Martha's reaction to Jesus' words, but we know she was confronted with an assessment of herself. She then had to decide what to do about it.

The same thing happens when we decide to evaluate our current ability to simplify our time. If we truly evaluate ourselves, we will find ourselves in a better place to make decisions that propel us to our goals.

Don't be afraid to find faults. When you find yourself at odds with your heart's desires, you are at a potential turning point. You see what you don't like in your life, and you can draw a line in the sand. On one side is the old way; on the other is the new, desired way.

> Take time to make an honest assessment of your situation. It may take an hour; it may take a day. Find a surrounding that helps you think. This could be a walk outdoors or a lounge chair with a fresh-brewed cup of coffee. Ask yourself, *Are the activities that fill my day aligned with my stated goals? Are they advancing or hindering the process? Does everything else line up with my goals?* Record your conclusions here.

When you are honest with yourself and clearly identify your faults, you're on the brink of change.

■ Time to Count on Others

Many people who try to make changes approach the adjustment with good intentions. But as time progresses, they slowly slide back into their old rut and find themselves living just as they did before. They also tend to rationalize their way out of self-imposed promises. At these times accountability to others can be indispensable. If we are serious about changing the way we use time, we need others who can watch our progress, who can recognize and verbalize the good and the bad, the aligned and the unaligned.

Follow these tips for choosing someone to hold you accountable for your actions.

1. Be picky. Steer away from family members. Seek an outsider.
2. Search for someone with goals similar to what you are trying to accomplish.
3. Make sure they hold the same values and will not hesitate calling you out when your actions no longer parallel your goals.
4. Set specific time intervals at which you will meet or speak, such as weekly or biweekly. Staying in contact is a must.

Name two persons you would consider to hold you accountable in aligning your life with your goals for using your time.

1.
2.

Ask God to show you who would be the better partner.

■ Time to Be Uniquely You

Can activities that align with your mission statement be wrong for you? Absolutely. When we start aligning our day to fit our mission statement and ultimately our heart's priorities, we will run into areas that go against our personalities.

God made each of us with different personalities, gifts, strengths, and weaknesses. Personality encompasses the total mix of who we are: our disposition, our background, our temperament, our talents, our spiritual gifts, and our personal history. Because everyone is wired differently, we can't expect everyone to align their lives the same way.

In the following pairs of words, check the one that best fits who you are.

☐ Steady   ☐ Fast
☐ Structured   ☐ Spontaneous
☐ Focused   ☐ Scattered
☐ Morning productive ☐ Evening productive
☐ Tense   ☐ Relaxed
☐ Hyper   ☐ Calm
☐ Talkative   ☐ Quiet
☐ Patient   ☐ Impatient
☐ Fun   ☐ Serious
☐ Compulsive   ☐ Thoughtful
☐ Competitive   ☐ Noncompetitive
☐ Worried   ☐ Hopeful

Now look at each of the words you checked. Does your mission statement fit the personality described by these words? Does it align with who you are? If not, what changes should you make in your statement?

Review what you have already done in the areas of clarity and movement. Do these previous steps fit who you are? Explain why or why not.

A key element of alignment is the proper fit. Embrace who God has made you and use it to mold your simple life.

Time to Stretch

Have you ever noticed that your life seems to be one big habit? You get up about the same time each day, alternate between the same two sugar-laden cereals for breakfast, and listen to the same radio station as you drive to work. The rest of your day generally follows a set routine. There is a rhythm to each of our lives, a beat that guides us throughout our day. But when the beat takes on a different rhythm, our day's dance becomes disrupted. We feel uncomfortable. Our life's waltz suddenly becomes the funky chicken. We are out of sync and awkward.

These uncomfortable feelings often push us to keep the rhythm, to do as we have always done. The simple life, however, requires flexibility. Life is not static. Therefore, your attempt to align will demand that you make changes. This may happen tomorrow; it may happen next year. Who knows where God may take you or what He may do with you?

Adopt an attitude of flexibility. What will happen if you stick with your ways, even when change is demanded? Life will continue to change with or without your permission. Staying ready for adjustment will help you capture the adventure of what a simple day can be.

How is aligning your life with your time goals requiring you to be flexible?

Relishing the Blemish

One of the beautiful things about a scar is that it demonstrates that healing took place. It represents an old wound from which we no longer suffer.

As we align our activities to move toward the simple life with our time, we should not expect perfection. We will probably find ourselves making mistakes, creating a few scars. But our response to those mistakes can be more important than the mistakes themselves. Will we allow them to become sources of frustration or inspiration?

Identify any unexpected struggles you have already had in trying to align your daily life with your goals for using time. Three ideas are suggested to get you started.

☐ I have leaned too much on my own strength and not on God's.
☐ I forgot to seek God's direction before trying to align.
☐ My plan didn't work.
☐ Other:

Because time has so many outside variables, mistakes can easily occur; alignment can easily become misalignment. We can't become so focused on the imperfections in this process that they hinder our advancement.

Allow your wounds, your mistakes, to heal. They heal when we step away from them and make a change. If you're lucky, a scar will remain. Use those scars as learning experiences, as markers of personal growth, lessons learned and survived.

How will you use the scars you already have in trying to change the way you use time?

You declared that you wanted to simplify your time, and you committed to action. We're sure it has not been easy. Change never is. We encourage you not to slow down but to keep passionately pursuing what your heart is telling you. In the end it will be something special.

Focus

■ **Day 5** Eliminating Some Good Time

The last step in simplifying our time is called focus. At this point in your process of simplification, you have done much to make sure your calendar matches your heart's desire. Each day's activities should reflect your priorities and move you toward your goals. But now it's time to ask, Are any activities weakening your ability to fulfill your mission statement, even though these activities reflect your priorities? In other words, is there ever too much of a good thing?

There is a point at which your good intention can become a burden. Although vacations are great, too many will make you broke and unemployed. While spending time with your spouse should be a main priority, too much will leave too little time for God and other important priorities in your life.

By now you know you need to cut out some things, but how do you know what to eliminate? The answer lies in establishing and maintaining focus. By creating an intentional focus, you enable your actions to be even more purposeful, more potent, and more direct.

simplelife   STATISTICS ■

50% *want to slow down, but they don't know how.*

■ The Fallout of Focus

In the story of Martha, we can imagine the frustration she must have felt when Jesus told her that her efforts focused on something that meant little and that Mary had chosen an act that meant everything. After all, Jesus taught His followers to be servants: "Whoever wants to become great among you must be your servant, and whoever wants to be first among you must be your slave" (Matt. 20:26-27).

> Why were Martha's servant actions inappropriate
> for the situation?

Maybe, for that moment, something took precedence over a good action.

During His time on the earth, Jesus was constantly aware of the brevity of His time living among us. With each passing day, with each step, and with each breath, Jesus was drawing closer to the cross. Like all of our lives, His life on earth was a constant march toward death. Unlike us, however, He knew the final hour, minute, and second. He therefore lived with an intentionality that we aren't capable of.

So maybe it wasn't that Martha's desire to serve was in itself wrong, but there was something greater to be done in that moment. These times with Jesus were fleeting, and He wanted her to spend time with Him while she had the opportunity. Sometimes even the best intentions may come up lacking if God is not in them.

As we focus our efforts on the mission alone, we must be willing to allow some good things to fall by the wayside. Sometimes the best thing we can do is to say no, not just to things that go against our priorities but also to activities that, while aligning with our priorities, actually push us further away from fulfilling our mission statement.

This leads us to a two-step process to increase your focus and the speed at which you can reach your goal.

■ Step 1: Be Willing to Let Go

In day 3 you eliminated bad areas of your life that did not line up with your priorities. In day 4 you made sure your activities matched the uniqueness of who you are. Letting go for the sake of focus is different. It is more difficult to let go of what truly lines up with your priorities but may still limit you in reaching your goal. Telling others you are limiting your overtime at work to free up more time to spend with your family is a lot different from announcing your plans to decrease your family time, even if it is to increase your time with God.

Focus is about completely purifying your actions so that nothing prevents you from simplifying your time. It's OK to step away from an activity, even if you are doing a good thing.

Don't get us wrong; doing good things is important to the Christian faith. The Book of James makes this clear. But it's very important that you seek God's direction in deciding what you need to let go of. Spend time in prayer asking Him to reveal to you whether these activities are to be abandoned, at least for a time.

Name some of the priorities you identified in your mission statement related to time.

Name some things you have eliminated or need to eliminate in order to work toward your goal.

Circle any good things that are keeping you from your goal.

If your goal is to have one meal a day with your family, do what is necessary to make this a priority. If your goal is to attend worship with your family, switch to another Bible study or otherwise alter your schedule to make this goal possible. There is a big difference between activities that have to be done and those that want to be done. Focus on what has to be done in order to simplify your time.

simplelife   STATISTICS ■

45% *of Christians rarely or never attend worship together as a family.*

■ Step 2: Discover Imbalance

We often hear from our culture that the best way to do life is to live a balanced one. It seems to us that many of our Bible heroes were quite unbalanced. They lived life in extremes. Yet it is because of their extremes that we talk about them today. Consider these examples.

- Noah built a massive wooden ship to house two of every kind of animal.
- John the Baptist lived in the desert, ate locusts and wild honey, and wore clothes of camel hair.
- Paul endured beatings, imprisonment, stoning, a shipwreck, hunger, and thirst for the sake of the gospel.

Some would probably say these men were a little unbalanced. But they were focused on the tasks God gave them to do.

Focus is by definition unbalanced. It is narrowing your field of vision so that you block out the unnecessary. Yet focus is powerful. When harnessing your energy for one or a few goals, your impact will be multiplied. Why is a laser so powerful? It is focused energy.

As you let go of certain things to gain focus, understand that you may lose some balance in your life. But also understand that balance is not always the best pursuit. It can sometimes spread you too thin with activities and make this journey more complex than it needs to be. It can cause you to have less of an impact.

Take hold of your priorities. Narrow your vision. Focus. Sure, you might become a little unbalanced, but you are in good company.

In what ways has your focus on your time goals brought imbalance to your life?

■ The Ultimate Story of Focus

There is no greater demonstration of focus than Jesus' example while on earth.

Read the following Scriptures.

"I have come down from heaven, not to do My will, but the will of Him who sent Me" (John 6:38).

"I have come that they may have life and have it in abundance" (John 10:10).

How did Jesus define His focus in John 6:38?

How did Jesus define His focus in John 10:10?

For 33 years Christ was placed on earth with one goal: to save the human race from sin. In His sight was the cross. That was His focus.

While on this earth, Jesus healed many people, exorcized many evil spirits, and raised people from the dead. But for all He did, the majority went without His help.

With all His power and authority, why do you think Jesus didn't reverse every sickness, every death, and every problem while He was on earth?

Jesus was on a divine schedule. From the moment of birth, His countdown began. Christ knew His main purpose was not to heal physical needs, because these healings would provide only temporal relief. He was sent to conquer the spiritual realm, a battle where the implications were eternal. So He set aside some healings and allowed some people to die. There was greater work to be done, work that was grossly misunderstood during His time on earth.

And we are left with an undeniable result: it worked. Jesus overcame what He was sent to overcome. He kept a laserlike focus on the battle between good and evil, life and death. And He won.

Some things are just more important than others. One good thing might be better than another good thing. It's OK to choose one over the other. In fact, it is critical. Stay focused; reach the goal.

Identify two or three things you still need to say no to, even if they are good things.

Write a concrete plan to eliminate some of the activities you have named.

Pause and pray for wisdom to discern the pace at which you need to eliminate things and for perseverance to follow through.

Let's review where you are on this time issue. Answer the questions in the four areas you have studied related to time.

Clarity

Do you have a plan for a better use of your time?
☐ Yes   ☐ No

Do you have a written mission statement to reflect that plan?
☐ Yes   ☐ No

Does your plan actually define the process you will use?
☐ Yes   ☐ No

Movement

What obstacles or impediments might hinder you from accomplishing your plan for a better use of your time?

What are you doing about these obstacles?

Alignment

Does your plan reflect who you are?   ☐ Yes   ☐ No
Your personality?   ☐ Yes   ☐ No
Your preferences?   ☐ Yes   ☐ No

What steps are you taking if you are out of alignment?

Focus

What good things do you need to eliminate from life?

The writer of Ecclesiastes said,

> There is an occasion for everything,
> and a time for every activity under heaven (Eccl. 3:1).

As part of God's purposeful creation, time has meaning for our lives here on earth. We discover that meaning as we submit our time to God and follow His direction for using it.

Truett Cathy built the successful Chick-fil-A® restaurant chain on Christian principles, values, and ethics. His decision to close the 1,200 restaurants on Sundays illustrated his recognition that some things matter more than business. Cathy once said, "I'd like to be remembered as one who kept my priorities in the right order. We live in a changing world, but we need to be reminded that the important things have not changed, and the important things will not change if we keep our priorities in proper order."[1]

You already know your time is important. Every day you walk a path without knowing when it will end. Your next step may be one of many or the very last. Each moment you have is precious. God has wired you to give priority to the heart. Make sure you don't leave this little, round rock called Earth without living out what God has placed on your heart.

Let your last breath be one of satisfaction, not regret.

It's all a matter of time.

1. "Truett Cathy quotes," *S. Truett Cathy* [online, cited 17 June 2009]. Available from the Internet: *www.truettcathy.com*.

How to Create and Keep Healthy Relationships

■ SESSION 3
Group Experience

1. Share insights from your time log on page 37. How well do your daily activities reflect the life priorities you recorded on page 36?
2. Identify any relational problems caused by your time challenges.

Clarity

1. Share the priorities for your life and the mission statement you recorded on pages 36 and 38.
2. Evaluate each mission statement against these criteria:

   • Does it reflect life priorities?
   • Is it clear and concise?
   • Does it include an action plan?
   • Is it realistic?

Movement

1. Identify choices you have made that interfere with your priorities.
2. How does self-absorption interfere with the simple life?
3. Share any barriers you have resolved to remove in your use of time.

Alignment

1. Share insights regarding the way you use time (p. 46). How well do your daily activities line up with your mission statement for time?
2. What struggles have you experienced in trying to align your daily life with your goals for time? What have you learned?

Focus

1. What good things are you doing that are preventing you from accomplishing your mission statement? How?
2. Share any commitments you have made to eliminate these things.

Can You Relate?

1. Show the DVD for session 3. Complete the viewer guide below.

How to Create and Keep Healthy Relationships

Congestion

_____

_____

The key to moving toward your goal is to make realistic, incremental _____.

2. Discuss Samantha's story. In what ways can you relate to her?
3. Share prayer concerns for your struggles with time. Pray silently that God will guide you to spend your time on things that have eternal value and that He will give you wisdom in choosing priorities.

Complete week 3 devotionals and activities before the next group session.

If you missed this session, go to www.lifeway.com/downloads to download this or any other session of Simple Life.

"I'm a terrible friend." We were surprised to hear those words from Samantha. The single 27-year-old certainly didn't seem to be a terrible person. We asked her to elaborate.

"I have three friends I am extremely close to. Two of them I have known since high school, and one I first met in college. Somehow, I guess through me, all four of us became really connected. We don't live that far from one another, but it would be at least a half-day drive for any of us. The point is, all of the others write one another and me. They are all good about calling. Most of them even make a point of visiting and getting together." She paused. "All of them but me."

"Is your schedule so busy that you don't have time to stay connected to your friends?"

"Well," she said pensively. "My schedule is incredibly busy, but I don't think I'm much busier than my friends. But somehow they make time to call me, send me e-mails, and even come see me. My best friend, Laura, sends me a handwritten note about once a month. She thinks she is encouraging me. If she only knew how guilty she was making me feel …" Then Samantha said it again: "I'm a terrible friend."

Samantha was agonizing over the way she treated her friends. She wasn't cruel or uncaring, but somehow she wasn't able to give them the priority she thought they deserved. At the same time, her friends always made time for her, which caused her to feel guilty and to realize that her priorities were out of balance.

This week you will have an opportunity to bring clarity to the priority of relationships in your life. You will identify the most important relationships to you and will discover how you can give attention to those relationships.

Clarity

■ Day 1 Making a Selfless Commitment

In 2008 the movie *Fireproof* was released. The central characters were firefighter Caleb Holt and his wife, Catherine. Caleb's rally cry each time he fought dangerous fires was "Never leave your partner." He practiced that principle with fidelity on the job.

The problem was his failure to live that principle in his marriage. The argumentative, strained relationship propelled the couple toward divorce. Catherine had enough, and Caleb was unwilling to fight for his marriage.

In a last-minute intervention Caleb's father challenged his son to fight for his marital partner with even more zeal than he would fight for his firefighting partner. His marriage and his wife were worth it, his dad explained. In the movie this challenge was called the love dare.

Fireproof tapped into a great need in our society. A hunger exists for healthier relationships not only between husbands and wives but also among fathers, mothers, sons, daughters, friends, and coworkers. Look at some of the comments from our surveys:

- "I would love for our family to spend more time together instead of needing to work so much and sending our son to day care."
- "I wish we could manage our time so that we could spend more weekends together."
- "I don't feel that I know my husband anymore. With our schedules we hardly even have time to talk."
- "I wish I had just one friend I could talk to anytime."
- "I need better relationships with my stepchildren. They really resent me."

- "We are constantly on the go due to our children's sporting events, and we hardly have any quality time together. We are gone from home almost every night of the week."
- "I have lots of people and family around me, but I'm so lonely."

Go back and place a check mark beside the respondents' comments that express the way you feel about your significant relationships.

This week we will look at the second of the big four needs we heard across our nation—relationships. What types of relationships need improving? We put them in three broad categories: spouses to one another, parents to children, and other relationships. Today we will examine the first category and identify ways you can bring clarity to your relationship with your spouse.

■ Seeking Healthier Relationships Between Husbands and Wives

You don't need statistics and data to know that many marriages are in trouble. As many as one in two marriages will end in divorce, and marriages after the first marriage have an even higher rate of failure. We could cite statistics on spouse abuse, separations in marriage, or spouses seeking crisis intervention in marriages.

But you don't need to be convinced. You see it in the news. You see it among your friends. Maybe you see it in your own home. Let's examine some of the reasons married couples need help with their relationships.

simple life   STATISTICS ■

42% *cannot strongly say they have a good marriage.*

84% *need to spend more time together.*

60% *would like their husbands or wives to demonstrate love to them.*

38% *are satisfied with the quality of their sex lives.*

33% *are satisfied with the frequency of sex in their marriages— 38% of wives and 27% of husbands.*

55% *of evangelical Christians are satisfied with their sex lives.*

Time. As we observed last week, time is a major issue. Married couples are time starved for each other.

Demonstrations of love. A lot of married couples know what they need to do, but they don't do it. For example, Shirley spoke for a lot of her friends when she said, "We would really like our husbands to demonstrate love to us as they did when we were dating and first married," she said straightforwardly. "Why can't there be romance after we've been married awhile?" Then Shirley looked at us right in the eyes. "What's wrong with you men?"

Shirley is both right and wrong. She is right that many spouses want their husbands and wives to demonstrate love to them. But she is wrong in assuming that the issue is just a cause for concern for wives. Men feel that way too. Activities have replaced demonstrations of love in too many marriages. That's not good.

What activities are getting in the way of your relationship with your spouse?

How are these activities affecting your relationship?

Read 1 John 3:18:

"Little children, we must not love in word or speech, but in deed and truth" (1 John 3:18).

Name one way your words have recently demonstrated love to your spouse.

Name one way your actions have recently demonstrated love to your spouse.

Satisfying sex life. In our research demonstrations of love were not limited to sex between husbands and wives, but sex is certainly a significant part of it. A large majority of married couples can't state strongly they are satisfied with the quality of their sex lives. And we see a direct relationship between this statistic and the problem Shirley identified. If romance and demonstrations of love are not taking place outside the bedroom, it is unlikely that romance in the bedroom is satisfying.

Meeting needs. What do spouses seek from each other? What can help the marriage grow stronger?

Read Ephesians 5:22-33. How did Paul say a wife should show love to her husband?

How is a husband to show love to his wife?

How do you and your spouse show love in these ways?

As we interviewed more than a thousand people, the married persons among the group were clear in what they would like from their spouses. The good news is that the requests are not unreasonable. The bad news is that the needs are largely unmet.

For example, husbands and wives would like their spouses to do little things for them. What are these little things? The responses were varied but predictable:

- "I wish he would help with just a little of the housework."
- "I would be happier if she showed more interest in my work."
- "Why can't she just try to enjoy watching one football game with me?"
- "I would love a shoulder rub without having to ask him."
- "Flowers. Unexpected. No special occasion."
- "We need to have more grown-up talk. All of our conversations are with the kids or about the kids."

List five things you would like your spouse to do for you.

1.
2.
3.
4.
5.

Now try to imagine what your spouse would like for you to do in the relationship.

1.
2.
3.
4.
5.

Here's the tough part. How many of the items on the second list are you willing to do for the other person if your spouse doesn't reciprocate? The way you answered will help you gauge your commitment to a selfless relationship.

simplelife   STATISTICS ■

40% *of married couples do little things for each other.*
36% *of married persons receive encouraging words from their spouses.*
36% *cannot say with certainty they would marry their current spouses again.*

Encouragement. Both husbands and wives long for words of affirmation and encouragement from their spouses. But only a minority strongly agree their spouses offer them words of encouragement.

You see, the simple life is really about simple things. And it's those simple things we neglect most.

Relationships become healthier when at least one of the parties has a selfless attitude. We challenge you to be selfless in your relationship with your spouse for a week to 10 days. Remember these points:

- Make the commitment for a brief time. Don't get too ambitious.
- To avoid failure, don't go overboard on what you'll do.
- Tell someone else about your commitment for accountability.
- Stay true to your commitment for a week even if the other person isn't responsive.

Name one thing you will do this week to demonstrate selflessness in your relationship.

Name one thing you will avoid doing.

Clarity

■ Parent-Child Relationships

Another type of relationship our study addressed was between parents and children. A majority of the respondents thought they had good relationships with their children. When we asked the question of the parents from the child's point of view ("My kids consider me to be a good parent"), the responses were identical. The majority of parents think they are doing a good job, and they believe their children would give the same assessment. So most parents think they are doing OK, but 4 of 10 parents really want to improve.

simplelife   STATISTICS ■

I am a good parent.
- **56%** *strongly agree.*
- **41%** *agree somewhat.*
- **3%** *disagree somewhat.*
- **0%** *strongly disagree.*

Check your response: I am a good parent.

☐ Strongly agree   ☐ Agree somewhat
☐ Disagree somewhat   ☐ Strongly disagree

In fact, when we changed the question to see how many parents were worried about how their children will turn out, the numbers indicate even more concern. Of course, these higher numbers reflect the reality that our children have free will, and even the best parents can have children who disappoint them.

simplelife STATISTICS ■

I am worried about how my kids will turn out.
29% *strongly agree.*
38% *agree somewhat.*
22% *disagree somewhat.*
10% *strongly disagree.*

When the question is rephrased to ask how parenting ultimately affects the lives of the children, the concerns are obviously higher. More than two-thirds of parents worry about their kids.

Check your response: I am worried about how my kids will turn out.

☐ Strongly agree   ☐ Agree somewhat
☐ Disagree somewhat   ☐ Strongly disagree

The comments and the interviews revealed some of the reasons for the concerns. One prominent issue, for example, was the common concern of lack of time, which we addressed last week. For example, Rebecca, a 33-year-old mother of two from Abilene, Texas, said, "My husband and I, as well as the two kids, are so busy with our own activities that we really don't have time for one another. It's kind of ironic. We want the best for our children, but we aren't giving them what they need the most—our time."

Fewer than one-third of parents strongly feel that they give their children enough time. Yet most of these same parents think they are working hard to be good parents. Their hectic schedule leaves them feeling exhausted, confused, and guilty.

Is your schedule keeping you from giving your children enough time? ☐ Yes ☐ No

If so, what is the effect on your relationship with your children?

Despite the seemingly best efforts of parents, they tell us they know their children less as the child gets older. Look at some of these disturbing results from our surveys.

simplelife   STATISTICS ■

I strongly feel that I really know my kids.
73% *When the oldest child is less than 6 years old*
58% *When the oldest child is 9 to 11*
48% *When the oldest child is 12 to 18*
43% *When the oldest child is 19 or older*

Check your response: I strongly feel that I really know my kids.

Birth to 6:	☐ Strongly agree	☐ Agree somewhat
	☐ Disagree somewhat	☐ Strongly disagree
9 to 11:	☐ Strongly agree	☐ Agree somewhat
	☐ Disagree somewhat	☐ Strongly disagree
12 to 18:	☐ Strongly agree	☐ Agree somewhat
	☐ Disagree somewhat	☐ Strongly disagree
19 and older:	☐ Strongly agree	☐ Agree somewhat
	☐ Disagree somewhat	☐ Strongly disagree

Parents tend to get their children involved in a plethora of activities at very young ages. But that busyness often does not provide the desired results. As the children get older, the parents feel less and less that they know their kids. Activities alone do not seem to provide healthier parent-child relationships. On the contrary, they may be at least partly responsible for doing just the opposite of the parents' dreams and wishes for their children.

Read Proverbs 1:8-9:

"Listen, my son, to your father's instruction,
and don't reject your mother's teaching,
for they will be a garland of grace on your head
and a gold chain around your neck" (Prov. 1:8-9).

Who is responsible for giving spiritual instruction to children?

The Bible makes it clear that parents are responsible for teaching their children about God and His ways. That's the best way to guarantee that kids will turn out all right. Proverbs 22:6 says,

Teach a youth about the way he should go;
even when he is old he will not depart from it.

■ Bringing Clarity to Your Relationships

As you recall, the first step in the simple life is the determination to move forward with clear, concrete action steps. Let us make some suggestions for bringing clarity to your relationships.

1. Decide what relationship you would like to improve. If you are dealing with multiple relationship issues, you need to work on just one at a time. Perhaps you can start with the relationship that gives you the most concern or the person closest to you. Which need is greatest?

Select the relationship you most need to work on.

☐ Husband ☐ Wife ☐ Child ☐ Parent ☐ Friend
☐ Coworker ☐ Neighbor ☐ In-law ☐ Other:

2. Define your "how" as well as your "what." Write a mission statement for improving the relationship you have chosen to focus on. Remember that a mission statement should have the following characteristics.

- It should be easy to understand. There must be no doubt about what you plan to do.
- It should be a process, including not only a declaration of your intentions but also steps to fulfill the intentions.
- It should be immediately doable. It should not be a lofty set of wishes you can't fulfill in the near future. Set your sights on something realistic and achievable.

Let's suppose Faye desires to improve her relationship with her husband, William. She then writes her mission statement:

I will strive to be a better wife to William.

That statement is doomed for failure because although it states the *what* (to have a better relationship with her husband), it does not state the *how* (the process she will take to accomplish her goal of being a better wife).

Instead, Faye's mission statement needs to define the *what* and the *how:*

I will be a better wife to William by giving him at least one compliment for the next 10 days and by not making any critical comments about him or to him during those same 10 days.

Now Faye is getting the job done. She not only has a mission statement that seeks to accomplish her goal, but she also has steps to accomplish that goal.

3. Don't overcommit yourself through your mission statement. Faye has made a commitment for 10 days. That's manageable. She has committed to pay at least one compliment to William each day. She can probably do that. And she has committed to refrain from criticizing her husband during this 10-day period. If she slips up, she can commit to getting it right the rest of the 10 days.

4. Find an accountability person. When you tell someone about your plans, you have created accountability. And that accountability increases your prospects for accomplishing the intent of your mission statement.

> Write your mission statement for the priority relationship you have identified.

So how did Faye do in executing her mission statement? She reported, "The process was amazing. I gave William at least one sincere compliment each day, usually two. I messed up on not criticizing two of the days, but I didn't let it stop me from keeping at it. I discovered two amazing things. First, selfless love and giving are so freeing. You don't give expecting anything in return. Second, I noticed a difference in William's attitude toward me after just three days. I think I like this so much, I will try something new soon."

Maybe we can help you bring about some changes in your relationships too. Tomorrow we're going from clarity to movement.

Movement

■ Day 3 Putting Relationships First

Shortly after Thom's dad and Art's grandfather, Sam, died, the family sat in the family room with Nan, the grieving widow. In a moment of silence someone asked Nan, "What do you already miss most about him?"

Nan did not hesitate to answer. Her response was quick and certain: "The flowers."

None of us were surprised. We understood. "The flowers."

During the long warm seasons in south Alabama, Sam was able to keep a healthy flower bed in his yard most months of the year. And each morning he would awaken early, go to the flower bed, and pick the most beautiful flower of the day. That flower was for Nan, the love of his life. It was his simple act of love.

When people described Sam Rainer as a simple man, they mean nothing but affirmation. He was extremely smart, near the top of his graduating class. He was both a bank president and the mayor in the small town where he lived all his life.

But Sam didn't need many things to be happy. He declined significant job offers in other towns. Why? He was happy in the small town. Why change for money or prestige? Some urged him to build a larger home. He declined. Why? The home he owned—1,600 square feet—had plenty of room. And when the town urged him to continue serving as mayor, he declined. Why? It was time for someone else to do the job. There were plenty of gifted people in town.

After all, he missed his hunting and fishing. With all of his responsibilities, he needed to be on the lake or in the woods more than when he was both mayor and bank president.

His was a simple life. And his was a good life.

Sam was never stingy with his family. On the contrary, he would give you anything you needed. He bought Nan things from time to time. But she did not mention the material items after he died. She missed the flowers.

Sam Rainer practiced and lived the simple life.

◼ Congestion and Relationships

Do you remember our earlier discussion of congestion? Congestion is caused by things that keep us from living the simple life and activities that keep us too busy to live the simple life. Congestion hinders relationships from developing to their full potential. It blocks the movement we must have to live the simple life. We are too busy in other areas of our lives to spend adequate time growing healthy relationships.

We heard it from more than a thousand respondents to our surveys. And we wouldn't be surprised if you readily identified with some of these comments:

- "Michelle and I always loved to spend a couple of hours talking each night when we first married. Now we are so busy taking the kids everywhere during the day that we are too tired to have much conversation at night."
- "I work more than 60 hours a week. I don't know where I will find time to connect with my friends. I'm barely connected to my family."
- "When we first married, Mark focused on the little things that meant so much to me. He would write me a note almost every week. Or he would bring me a single flower. Now that we've been married three years, he's stopped doing those little things."
- "Sometimes I wish I was a football game so that Jeremy would give me that kind of attention."
- "I try to stay in touch with Susan, but she doesn't reciprocate. I'm about to give up on her."

Scripture is clear about the obstacles believers need to remove from our relationships. Because Christ lives in us, we are a new creation (see 2 Cor. 5:17). Paul admonishes us to live by the new nature as we cast off the old ways of the flesh.

Read Colossians 3:5-14. List in the appropriate column what qualities we are to put off and what qualities we are to put on.

Put Off

Put On

_____ _____
_____ _____
_____ _____
_____ _____
_____ _____
_____ _____
_____ _____

Yesterday you wrote a mission statement for a significant relationship in your life. Several things, however, can keep you from moving toward your goal.

- Busyness with other activities
- Exhaustion from doing so many other things
- The pursuit or enjoyment of material things

These obstacles are examples of congestion. To simplify relationships, movement must follow clarity.

■ Recognize the Congestion of Activities

Activities are replacing purpose in too many of our lives. We are so busy doing things that we are neglecting the things that really matter. Often, activities replace important matters that help relationships grow. Busyness causes us to hurt others and hinders healthy relationships.

In responding to our surveys, spouses and parents didn't say they needed to provide more material items for their loved ones or more activities in order to enjoy the good life. In fact, in our surveys we heard little about buying nicer cars, getting children more involved in sports, working longer hours, or buying bigger homes. Instead, we typically heard that these items made life congested. They caused blockage that prevented movement toward the simple life.

simplelife   STATISTICS ■

33% *say their lives are too busy.*

75% *either state clearly that they are too busy or are unable to say they aren't too busy.*

13% *strongly agree that family members can relax and enjoy one another.*

List things and activities that prevent you from spending time with the people you care about.

How are these things damaging your relationships?

What relationships are being affected?

What adjustments would give you more time to improve your relationships?

We know what we need to do. But we aren't doing it.

Clarity is the intention. Movement is the action.

■ Recognize the Congestion of Selfishness

One of the most common types of congestion in developing relationships is selfishness. Instead of seeking the best for the other person, you look at the relationship from the lens of what the other person can and should do for you.

When the apostle Paul wrote his first letter to the Corinthian church, he was dealing with a pretty self-centered congregation. In 1 Corinthians 13 Paul warned the Corinthians to cease their selfish ramblings and to start practicing selfless love toward one another. Paul's description of true, unconditional love teaches us how to relate to one another selflessly.

Read 1 Corinthians 13. Then as you read about the following characteristics of selfless love, underline statements that indicate movement you need to make in your life.

Love is patient (v. 4). Consider the inverse of this description: love is not impatient. If you sometimes lose patience with a spouse, child, coworker, or friend, you are seeking your own desires and needs before those of others. Patient love always places someone else's needs before your own.

Love is kind (v. 4). Kindness implies intentionality. When you are kind to someone, you make an overt effort to do a good deed or to say a positive word about him or her. Kindness typically requires forethought, and that forethought is an effort itself to demonstrate love. The very act of thinking about what you can do for someone else is a selfless act.

Love does not envy (v. 4). "I want only the best for my wife." The speaker's wife totally disagreed. "You say you want the best for me," she told her husband, "but your actions say otherwise. I can't remember the last time you asked me what I would like to do or where I'd like to go. You seem to resent the idea of my enjoying myself."

What if you looked at relationships through the lens of wanting only the best for the other person? Congestion occurs in your relationships when you envy others.

Love is not boastful (v. 4). We know someone who has been pretty successful, at least by the world's standards. And we admit, he has some pretty impressive accomplishments. But do you know what else we noticed about him? He has no friends. As a matter of fact, we don't enjoy being around him either. Why? He always talks about himself and what he has accomplished. The only people who stay around him are eager sycophants, not real friends. Love does not seek to dominate the conversation with self. Love is eager to hear from others.

Love is not conceited (v. 4). This comment is parallel to Paul's comment about boasting. When you boast, you talk about yourself. When you are conceited, you focus on yourself. But love is concerned about others.

Love does not act improperly (v. 5). Some translations say, "Love is not rude." At the heart of rudeness or acting improperly is a disregard for others. This lack of love is also a lack of respect for another person.

Love is not selfish (v. 5). Our surveys indicated that selfishness is pervasive in many relationships. We rarely heard a spouse say he or she should do more for the other spouse. Movement toward the simple life is not taking place in many relationships because so many look out only for their own needs.

Love is not provoked (v. 5). Sometimes anger is appropriate. Jesus was angry when He saw hardness of heart (see Mark 3:5) and money changers in the temple (see John 2:14-17). But this text speaks to those who are easily angered, hotheaded people whose tempers are ignited over small things. That type of quick anger focuses on self and shows an unwillingness to be patient.

Love does not keep a record of wrongs (v. 5). In the Book of Hosea, God instructed the prophet Hosea to take Gomer as his wife even though she was a promiscuous woman. God then told Hosea to take back his wife again and again even though she was unfaithful. Hosea received this burden from God to show God's forgiving love to the unfaithful Israelites.

But that persistent, forgiving love should be part of our lives as well. We often feel more justified when we hold grudges and refuse to forgive. After all, that person wronged us. Why should we even think about forgiving him or her? But the apostle Paul said love keeps no record of wrongs.

Sometimes relationships are hindered because we have an unforgiving spirit, even though we were wronged. That's tough to remedy. But it's mandatory, and it's biblical.

Go back and note areas that indicate movement you need to make in your relationships. Spend time in prayer asking God to change your heart to be more loving. Ask Him to forgive your failures in loving others as you should. Identify one thing you can do to express love in your relationships.

■ Incremental Movement

Remember Faye from yesterday? She wrote this mission statement about her relationship with her husband:

I will be a better wife to William by giving him at least one compliment for the next 10 days and by not making any critical comments about him or to him during those same 10 days.

The key to creating movement toward your relational goal is to make realistic, incremental steps. Faye's goal of complimenting William once a day was doable. Begin by making a small commitment, as Faye did. Hers was one compliment a day for 10 days. It's reasonable. It's doable. It's incremental.

Review your relational mission statement on page 74.
Identify one step you can take to move toward your goal.

We realize that in 7 to 10 days you won't go from where you are to where you need to be in relationships. But you will make progress. That's how you have movement toward the simple life. That's how you begin the steps toward healthier relationships.

Tomorrow we will explore whether the values and actions in your life are well aligned so that you can accomplish your goals.

Alignment

You have looked at the concept of clarity in relationships, and you have written a mission statement for a significant relationship in your life. You have identified obstacles to growth in your relationships and ways to move beyond this congestion. Now you are ready for alignment, making certain that all you do moves you toward the accomplishment of your purpose.

Goals cannot be accomplished and missions cannot be fulfilled when persons in relationships are not aligned with each other. In relationships the failure to align usually doesn't mean one party is right and the other party is wrong. Instead, it could mean that persons in a relationship see things from different perspectives.

In our surveys of more than a thousand men and women across America, we found that many times relationships were solid because people were all on the same page. Husbands and wives saw things from the same perspective. Friends had similar values. Coworkers had common goals. And neighbors saw the same needs in their neighborhood. If we don't acknowledge the reality of different perspectives, they can keep relationships out of alignment. Let's look at some common reasons alignment doesn't take place in relationships.

Men and Women *Are* from Different Planets

Many times male and female perspectives are vastly different, so often both parties know they are right and the other person is wrong. Yet we found that the issue is more often one of perspective.

The gender breakdown for our study was 465 males and 612 females. Though the females had an edge in the number of respondents

(57 percent to 43 percent), the sample size of each gender group was sufficient to give us some pretty fascinating insights into the different perspectives between men and women.

simple life   STATISTICS ■

40% *of mothers feel they spend enough time with their children.*
20% *of fathers feel they spend enough time with their children.*
55% *of mothers feel they know their children.*
47% *of fathers feel they know their children.*
45% *of mothers feel it is important to teach their children how to have a relationship with God.*
31% *of fathers feel it is important to teach their children how to have a relationship with God.*
68% *of mothers make efforts to be better parents.*
59% *of fathers make efforts to be better parents.*

For example, let's look at the relationships between mothers and children and then fathers and children. Although few parents believe they are perfect in their parenting skills, mothers are more likely than fathers to be confident that they are doing OK. The percentage of mothers who strongly agreed they were spending enough one-on-one time with their children was double the percentage of fathers who expressed strong agreement with that statement. That difference is statistically significant and relationally staggering. Fathers were also more likely to sacrifice family for work, while working moms tended to sacrifice work for family.

When we asked both parents whether they knew their children well, the responses were not surprising. Because mothers were more likely to give time to their children, they were also more likely to know their children well.

Generally, the women in the study tended to be more religious, and more were specifically Christian than men. It is therefore no surprise that the females in our study were more likely to teach their children how to have a relationship with God. Again, the difference between the two is significant both statistically and relationally. These responses show that men and women have different perspectives on parenting.

Discuss with your spouse your views of the following areas of parenting and note ways your responses differ.

Parenting skills:

Amount of time you spend with your children:

Spiritual instruction of the children:

Efforts to be a better parent:

Identify and discuss any adjustments the two of you can make to align your parenting with your goals for the children.

Gender differences are not limited to parenting perspectives in relationships. They also hold true for views of the strength of the marriage, perceptions of physical affection, and quality of sex life.

simplelife   STATISTICS ■

62% *of wives strongly agree they have a strong marriage.*

54% *of husbands strongly agree they have a strong marriage.*

51% *of wives strongly agree their spouse is physically affectionate.*

40% *of husbands strongly agree their spouse is physically affectionate.*

41% *of wives are satisfied with the quality of their sex lives.*

35% *of husbands are satisfied with the quality of their sex lives.*

Plan private time with your spouse in which you discuss your level of satisfaction with the emotional and physical intimacy in your marriage. What adjustments need to be made?

These statistics reinforce the obvious: men and women are different. They have different perspectives and different needs. Sometimes they are on the same page, but oftentimes they are not. We are not suggesting that relationship alignment means men and women should become relational clones. On the contrary, we celebrate our differences. But we are suggesting that men and women should be aware of and appreciate their differences. In dating relationships. In marriages. In sibling relationships.

■ Faith Misalignment

Our research gives a glimpse of the problems that can occur when matters of faith become misaligned. In our surveys approximately 79 percent said they were Christians, while 21 percent said they were not Christians. The differences between the two groups were significant on relationship issues, particularly when it comes to teaching children about God and moral values.

simplelife

79% *are Christians.*

21% *are not Christians.*

45% *of Christian parents teach their children how to have a relationship with God.*

14% *of non-Christian parents teach their children how to have a relationship with God.*

83% *of Christians strongly agree they should teach moral values to their children.*

77% *of non-Christians strongly agree they should teach moral values to their children.*

76% *of Christians strongly agree they will stay married to their current spouse until one of them dies.*

64% *of non-Christians strongly agree they will stay married to their current spouse until one of them dies.*

38% *of Christians believe their children should attend a weekly worship service.*

9% *of non-Christians believe their children should attend a weekly worship service.*

61% *of Christians strongly agree they have a strong marriage.*

49% *of non-Christians strongly agree they have a strong marriage.*

59% *of Christians strongly assess their parenting skills as good.*

47% *of non-Christians strongly assess their parenting skills as good.*

Our research clearly indicates that those who identify themselves as Christians often have a different perspective on relationships than those who do not. The danger for misalignment is great in areas like the following.

- Commitment to stay married to current spouse until one of them dies
- Need to bring children to a weekly worship service
- Tendency to have a strong marriage
- Tendency to have strong parenting skills

Consider the relationship about which you wrote your relational mission statement on page 74. Is there faith misalignment between the two of you? If so, what problems are being created?

Persons of faith align their actions with the teachings of Scripture. Read Romans 12:9-21 and check the behaviors and attributes that believers need to demonstrate in their relationships with others.

☐ Be patient.   ☐ Show brotherly love.
☐ Show honor.   ☐ Serve your own interests.
☐ Rejoice in hope.   ☐ Detest evil; cling to good.
☐ Persist in prayer.   ☐ Share with others.
☐ Avenge yourself.   ☐ Cultivate pride.
☐ Live at peace.   ☐ Curse those who persecute you.

■ Commitment Inconsistencies

Misalignment occurs in a relationship when one or both parties are not truly committed to the relationship. We saw some correlation between demographic profiles and the level of commitment to a marriage. For example, when we asked the respondents whether they would marry their same spouse if they had to do it over again, the differences were significant. More wives than husbands strongly agreed they would marry the same spouse if they could do it over again. Overall, one of three married persons expressed doubt they would marry the same person if they had the chance to do it over again.

simplelife   STATISTICS ■

69% *of wives strongly agree they would marry the same spouse again.*
60% *of husbands strongly agree they would marry the same spouse again.*
66% *of Christians strongly agree they would marry the same spouse.*
54% *of non-Christians strongly agree they would marry the same spouse.*

The simple life in relationships requires alignment. Unfortunately, many marriages aren't aligned because commitment is lacking.

This commitment issue is not limited just to marriages. The same issue is present in other relationships as well. Alignment can't take place in relationships unless there is true commitment.

Rate your commitment level to the following relationships in your life, with 1 being low and 5 being high.

Spouse   1 2 3 4 5

Children   1 2 3 4 5

Parents   1 2 3 4 5

Best friend   1 2 3 4 5

Boss   1 2 3 4 5

Coworkers   1 2 3 4 5

■ The Time Issue

Misalignment in relationships also takes place if there is not sufficient time for the relationship to grow. Because we studied time and the simple life last week, we will not stay on this point long.

Of all the married persons in our surveys, 43 percent strongly agreed and 41 percent somewhat agreed they needed to spend more time with their husbands or wives. Simple math tells us that 84 percent is a pretty strong indicator.

Relationships are misaligned if there is not sufficient time for them to grow. Simple enough.

Name one thing you can do to have more time for the relationship you have chosen to focus on this week.

■ The Money Issue

Money differences and money problems can really cause problems in relationships, particularly within immediate families. Volumes have been written about it. Seminars abound. People make their living advising about it. But money problems still exist. In fact, money problems are pervasive. It's such an important issue for the simple life that we will devote a whole week's study to it (week 4).

Focus

The simple life requires focus in relationships. Sounds simple, doesn't it? Hardly.

Focus requires that we abandon everything that interferes with developing the best possible relationships. That means not just letting go of the bad stuff in our lives. It includes eliminating the not-so-bad stuff and even some good stuff. It's possible to become so overcommitted to many good things that we do few of them well, including relating to others.

Developing healthy relationships as part of the simple life requires sacrifice. What areas of your life might require sacrifice? Let's look at a few possibilities.

■ Sacrificing the Material for the Relational

In the movie *Fireproof,* alluded to earlier this week, Caleb is the neglectful and self-centered husband who verbally abuses his wife, Catherine. One of his primary goals in life is to buy the boat of his dreams. But he finally discovers that the boat can't be his source of happiness. He gives his hard-earned savings to Catherine's parents, who have medical and financial needs. When Caleb sacrifices his desire for the good of others, he finds true joy.

simple**life** STATISTICS ■

13% *have incomes below $20,000.*
24% *have incomes below $30,000.*
15% *have incomes above $100,000.*
28% *strongly agree they are living within their financial means.*
80% *are concerned about their level of debt.*
5% *feel they are saving enough money.*

We found in our surveys that many people were chasing the material at the expense of the relational. And they weren't happy. We clearly heard that the material world was not bringing joy to families. On the contrary, the pursuit of material possessions often came at the expense of relationships.

Perhaps too many things are keeping you from closer relationships. Perhaps you are pursuing those things through long hours and tiring work. As a consequence, you have little time for the relationships that really matter.

The material items you possess and the long hours you work are not examples of bad character, unless they interfere with what really matters. Like relationships. If so, it's time to focus. Time to eliminate. Time to sacrifice.

■ Sacrificing Self-Focus for Other-Focus

One of the greatest needs we have in all relationships is to focus on others. The apostle Paul said, "Do nothing out of rivalry or conceit, but in humility consider others as more important than yourselves. Everyone should look out not only for his own interests, but also for the interests of others" (Phil. 2:3-4). The simple life means we sacrifice self for others. It means we are highly intentional about serving others. We should put others' needs before our own.

Two of Jesus' disciples presented Him an interesting opportunity to teach about the importance of serving others.

Read Matthew 20:20-28. What was James and John's mother seeking?

What did Jesus mean by "the cup that I am about to drink" (v. 22)?

What did Jesus identify as the key to greatness?

Jesus turned the tables upside down for the disciples. As they were seeking fulfillment through power and prestige, He told them a meaningful life is possible only when we put others before ourselves. The cross that was to come, the ransom for many, was to be the supreme example of self-giving.

Many relationships are suffering because one or both parties are focused on self. Only about one-third of the respondents strongly agreed that their spouses offer them words of encouragement. And nearly 100 percent wished they did. The problem is present in all relationships, not just the marriage relationship.

Perhaps the relationship needs more focus. And focus means we are willing to eliminate some things, even if those things aren't bad in themselves.

Ascertain your self-focus or other-focus by honestly responding to the following questions.

Could I eliminate some activities that focus on my needs and desires so that I can give attention to others?   ☐ Yes   ☐ No
Do I often focus on what the other person should do for me instead of what I could do for him or her?   ☐ Yes   ☐ No

Is my pursuit of material gain and higher position coming at the cost of relationships? ☐ Yes ☐ No

Am I angry with someone because of what they haven't done for me? ☐ Yes ☐ No

Do I intentionally do something sacrificially for someone each day? ☐ Yes ☐ No

Do others honestly see me as selfish or selfless? ☐ Selfish ☐ Selfless

■ Sacrificing Busyness for Relationships

As we discovered in week 1, busyness creates relational problems. The simple life demands that you focus by eliminating much of your busyness. Your relationship with someone you care about is simply too important to keep doing all you've been doing.

simplelife   STATISTICS ■

13% *strongly agree their families have enough relaxing times together.*

40% *say they are on emotional edge because of their schedules.*

25% *strongly agree they need to spend relaxed time with their children.*

■ Five Questions for Focus

Focus is usually the most difficult step to execute. Although we don't offer a magic bullet, we are proposing some questions that can help you sharpen your focus.

If the party in your relationship could change some things about your life, what would they be? Allen was surprised to learn that his wife wanted him to get back into teaching. His income would be less, but she knew he would be most fulfilled this way. And she knew his happiness affected all of the family.

Focus may seem to be an unrealistic goal because we think some things in our lives just can't be eliminated. Have you considered asking someone close to you? You may be surprised by their suggestions for improving your life and relationships.

Could you eliminate a material possession that may be hindering a relationship? We know a guy who loved boating. Guess what he did recently? He sold his boat. Nothing was inherently wrong with boating, but he discovered he was so busy with those activities that he was neglecting his wife and two children. By selling that one possession, he made a major step toward the simple life.

Could you eliminate a job? Now that really sounds radical. But plenty of people have done it. Your current job may be interfering with your relationships by taking too much of your time or by keeping you on edge. A lack of happiness and fulfillment in our vocations affects our relationships. But sadly, most people live with the pain and drudgery of an unfulfilling job. Changing jobs may be necessary to simplify your life and improve your relationships.

Are any casual activities interfering with your relationships? Some of us are addicted to the e-world. Others spend hours watching television. Some are totally consumed with sports. And others usually have their noses in books, newspapers, and magazines. At best these are distractions from healthy relationships. At worst these casual activities may be causing deep fissures in relationships. Are there casual activities you need to eliminate or reduce?

Would your children like to eliminate some of their activities? If you still have children at home, have you looked at their activities lately? Are they busy? Are they too busy? Try asking them if they would they change their activities if they could and what changes they would make.

Granted, we can't do everything our kids ask us. Many of them might eliminate school. Not a good option.

Still, you might be surprised by their choices. You may have them involved in activities for their own good, only to find they're really not happy with what they're doing. When they are better focused, the parents can be better focused as well.

Pray about any of the following things or activities you can eliminate to focus on your goal of healthier relationships. Write anything the Lord brings to mind.

Changes the other person in the relationship might suggest:

A material possession:

A job:

Casual activities:

Activities your children might need to eliminate:

■ What Really Matters

Jesus said, "Love the Lord your God with all your heart, with all your soul, and with all your mind. This is the greatest and most important commandment. The second is like it: Love your neighbor as yourself" (Matt. 22:37-39).

It's really simple, Jesus said. The most important thing that matters is our relationship with God. And the second most important thing that matters is our relationships with others. We need to focus to give attention to these things.

That's the simple life.

And that's what really matters.

How to Simplify and Build Healthy Finances

■ SESSION 4
Group Experience

1. Share what you learned from the activity on pages 67–68.
2. What keeps you from spending more time with your spouse?
3. What keeps you from giving your children adequate quality time?

Clarity

1. Share the mission statement you wrote for the relationship you desire to improve (p. 74).
2. Evaluate each mission statement against these criteria:

   - Does it reflect life priorities?
   - Is it clear and concise?
   - Does it include an action plan?
   - Is it realistic?

Movement

1. How does congestion hinder healthy relationships?
2. Read Colossians 3:5-14. Name the obstacles to healthy relationships and the qualities that contribute to healthy relationships.
3. What activities keep you from developing healthier relationships?

Alignment

1. How can faith misalignment cause problems in a relationship?
2. Read Romans 12:9-21. How can alignment with these biblical attributes and behaviors strengthen a relationship?

Focus

1. Read Philippians 2:3-4. How can you intentionally serve the person you have chosen as your relationship of focus this week?
2. Share activities you have committed to eliminate for the sake of your significant relationships.

Money Matters

1. Show the DVD for session 4. Complete the viewer guide below.

How to Simplify and Build Healthy Finances

The _____

The _____

The _____ Future

Qualifications for an Accountability Partner

They must understand your _____ goals.

They must have similar _____.

They must understand _____ at a basic level.

They must be willing to provide _____ feedback.

They cannot be a _____ member.

Aligning Your Finances

Your finances need to fit your _____.

Be willing to make _____ and accept imperfection.

2. Discuss Josh's story. In what ways can you relate to him?
3. Share prayer concerns about your relationships. Take turns praying for specific needs as you seek to love others as Jesus did.

Complete week 4 devotionals and activities before the next group session.

If you missed this session, go to www.lifeway.com/downloads to download this or any other session of Simple Life.

The coffee bar near the university was a little more crowded than usual, but Josh found a seat in the corner. As the students talked and laughed, Josh reminisced about his college years. Life seemed so simple then. The future was wide open, and money was not an issue.

Josh couldn't help but think how much life had changed. He wondered how he was going to dig out of the hole in which he and Elaine found themselves. Josh didn't want to become one of those people who were unable to pay their bills, but he was getting close. Because of an increase in interest rates, his mortgage payment had just been adjusted by a couple of hundred dollars more per month. The credit-card balances they swore would be paid off before the 0 percent interest offer ended were still there, now with a looming double-digit rate. He didn't even want to think how many more years of lease payments they had on their cars.

Josh and Elaine were also wrestling with the decision of whether they could pay for their daughter's cheerleading trip. They didn't want to be the types of parents who limited their children's dreams. "Man, I need some more money," Josh mumbled to himself. Before leaving, he went to the counter and asked, "Are you guys hiring?"

Josh walked out of the coffee bar with application in hand and a lingering sense of embarrassment. Did he really just ask for this?

Do you agree that Josh needs more money to solve his financial problems? Or do you see other solutions in his story? What about your own financial situation? This week you will discover how the principles of the simple life apply to the crazy world of finances. The Bible has a lot to say about this subject, and it may surprise you to learn how much clarity it can bring to the way you spend and manage money.

Clarity

■ Why We Hate Finances

Finances can seem like such a dirty word. It always carries baggage. For many of us it's like bitter taste in the mouth, reminding us of previous or current money problems. We tell ourselves there are more important things in life than money. Yet we still find it difficult to ignore the abundance of teachings in Scripture about finance. Money was one of Jesus' most frequent topics of discussion. We hate finances, but we know they are important in our life's journey.

Here are some quotations from the respondents to our surveys.

- "I would like to have complete financial freedom without worrying about any money matters."
- "We need to pay down a lot of debt."
- "I would love to know that my kids and I would have no worries when it comes to money in the future."
- "I wish I could afford to quit my second job and spend more time with the family."

simplelife   STATISTICS ■

45% *don't have enough income for their lifestyles.*
50% *say finances cause strain in their marriages.*
60% *indicate that finances are causing significant stress in their families.*

For many of us, money is a ball and chain that limits our life's movement. We feel that if we could just get a few extra zeros added to our bank account, then maybe the weight would start to lighten. Those who have had financial trouble can attest to the amount of stress it places on them and their families. What do we do? Which bill do we pay? How are we going to pay for the kids' education? What's going to happen to us?

List any symptoms of financial stress in your life.

What do you see as the greatest financial need in your life?

The complexity of finances doesn't help—credit scores, amortization schedules, interest rates, total cost of funds, budgeting, stocks, mutual funds, IRAs, and investment strategies.

It's also easy to get lost in a fog of confusing, conflicting messages about money. Everyone—from banks to retailers to credit-card companies—seems to know what our money should be used for except us.

What are we trying to accomplish with our money? As with our time and relationships, we need clarity about our finances.

■ Making Finances Simple

Let's try to bring clarity to our situation by examining a story Jesus told about a master and his three servants.

Read Matthew 25:14-30. What were the master's expectations of his servants?

What did the servants do with their money?

The first servant turned five talents into _____.

The second turned two talents into _____.

What did the third servant do?

Jesus' story provides clarity in our fiscal haze. Finding financial clarity requires a big idea, an all-encompassing direction from which we can make monetary decisions: Should I buy this? Should I invest in that? Should I pay this off first? Can I splurge on this? There are a lot of questions out there, each with their own nuances. And just one idea offers answers for them all: stewardship. It's the only concept that provides clarity for our finances.

Based on Jesus' story, how would you define *stewardship?*

Much like the servants in Jesus' story, a steward is traditionally someone who takes care of another's household. A steward manages the domestic affairs so that the master can focus on whatever he deems most important. The master therefore places a great deal of trust in the steward, whom the master expects to act in his best interest, with or without his oversight. So stewardship consists of managing the obligations given to the steward.

By the very nature of the word, stewardship requires some type of higher authority. It involves submission to a greater good. It is denying yourself and exalting another. It is commitment to the well-being of another, knowing their happiness will result in your happiness.

Ultimately, Jesus' story addresses stewardship on a much larger scale than money. It's about God calling all of us to take care of His things while we are on this brief journey in life. And though this chapter is about money, the concept of stewardship reaches far beyond the boundaries of our bank account. Everything we have and everything we are belong to the One who created us. Our entire being demands stewardship.

Why does God want us to be guardians of His money? So that His will is done on earth as it is in heaven. For God to give the title of steward to us, His own creation, is remarkable. In an incredible twist, God, perfect and righteous, has chosen us fallible and sometimes idiotic humans to watch over His resources until He returns. Knowing our imperfections, He still put together a human portfolio in which He would invest to accomplish His goals.

Read 1 Timothy 6:10.

"The love of money is a root of all kinds of evil, and by craving it, some have wandered away from the faith and pierced themselves with many pains" (1 Tim. 6:10).

Check the correct responses.

☐ Money is the root of evil.
☐ The love of money is a root of all kinds of evil.
☐ Craving money leads people away from God and brings suffering.

Money in itself is not evil. When properly utilized, it can produce all kinds of good in our world. On the other hand, money makes a poor god. If we fail to be good stewards of the money God gives us, many of our financial decisions reduce the potential impact we can have on this earth. They can diminish our fulfillment as God's agents of change.

Jesus said, "Collect for yourselves treasures in heaven, where neither moth nor rust destroys, and where thieves don't break in and steal. For where your treasure is, there your heart will be also" (Matt. 6:20-21). Stewardship is not a mathematical formula or a list of do's and don'ts. Stewardship is about the heart. It's about waking up every morning ready to listen to what God wants us to do for the day. It's about wanting to take care of what God has given us while we are on this little blue planet. It's about acknowledging that His plan is much greater than anything we could imagine. It's about being willing to make financial decisions based on His wants and not ours. Financial clarity is possible only for a steward who stubbornly tries to capture God's desires for His resources.

Based on the previous descriptions of stewardship, would you describe yourself as a good steward of God's resources?
☐ Yes   ☐ No

Why or why not?

Clarity

■ Components of Stewardship

There are two critical qualities of a steward: detachment and wisdom. Though a caretaker is intimately involved in the affairs of his master, he must never begin to think the possessions he watches are his own. He cannot allow himself to consider that he deserves all he oversees and to dub himself the rightful title owner. Only when the steward is completely detached from his master's belongings is he able to determine how his master's property can be used most productively. And the quality of wisdom ensures that a steward gives priority to what is most important to His master.

Read Mark 10:17-22. Why did this man come to Jesus?

What kept the man from obtaining eternal life? Check one.

☐ Disobedience to the law
☐ Attachment to money and possessions
☐ Failure to honor his father and mother

Ephesians 2:8-9 says eternal life is by grace, not by works. Why did Jesus tell the man he must sell his possessions to inherit eternal life?

Depressing. The young man had just looked Christ in the eyes, and though no words were spoken, he made his answer clear. His attachment to money and possessions twisted his decision making so much that, although he looked directly into the face of salvation, he turned and walked away. The primary rules of stewardship had been broken. Here was a man without detachment and wisdom.

After Jesus told him to get rid of his wealth, the man went away grieving. Jesus' words broke his heart. He could not envision a life without all of the luxuries to which he had become accustomed. On one side of the scale were earthly riches; on the other side stood Jesus. And he made his choice. The attraction and comfort of wealth were too strong for the young man.

Identify a time when money or a material possession distorted your priorities.

How did God bring clarity and help you restore balance?

■ Your Financial Statement

Our study indicated that many are in dire need just to get the basics in order. We can't know your greatest financial needs. Maybe you need to get out of debt or save for retirement. Instead of taking a more traditional path of setting up a budget and making long-term financial plans, you will begin by deciding your financial purpose. By now you understand the importance of creating a mission statement that sets the direction for each critical area of your life. Whatever your financial situation, your statement must be piloted by stewardship. Stewardship will guide you through the movement, alignment, and focus phases until you have simplified your financial picture. You will approach financial issues as a steward of God's resources.

Let's start working on that statement. Three categories of finance need to be addressed.

The Now (0–10 years). These financial concerns will impact our immediate to 10-year time horizon. Some of these concerns may be bills, credit cards, short-term loans, or emergency funds.

The Future (10+ years). These decisions will affect our lives beyond this decade. For many people these include retirement, college funds, and mortgages.

The Far Future (your legacy). Proverbs 13:22 indicates that the finale of one's relationship with money comes at death:

> A good man leaves an inheritance to his grandchildren,
> but the sinner's wealth is stored up for the righteous
> (Prov. 13:22).

When we pass away, we can leave an inheritance for the next generation. Sometimes this consideration doesn't make it into financial planning, but it is imperative for Christians. Even in death we demonstrate our love for others.

Of course, as we move through life, our financial concerns evolve. The decisions for the Future, such as retirement and advance fund planning, may become part of the Now as they develop into an immediate concern. As circumstances change, so will our finances.

Before developing your financial mission statement, list and rank your financial goals in the following categories. This is the time to paint your ideal financial picture. Have fun with it, but be realistic. That 55-foot yacht can wait until you tackle some more important issues.

The Now:

The Future:

The Far Future:

Recall Josh at the beginning of the week (p. 100). The contemplative coffee drinker knew his finances were out of control. He felt the despair and stress of an increasingly overwhelming burden from past financial decisions. Here is what he wrote:

The Now
1. *Give back to God.*
2. *Pay off credit cards.*
3. *Have more available money each month.*
4. *Create an emergency fund.*

The Future
1. *Retire at 65.*
2. *Pay for kids' college.*
3. *Be mortgage-free.*

The Far Future
1. Have enough life insurance to care for family.
2. Give each child $200,000 at death.
3. Have a will.

Of course, if you are married, be sure to discuss and develop your goals together. You might be surprised to find that your spouse's big financial priority is not your own. A married couple should have only one list of priorities. Finances will continue to be strained if the couple can't agree on priorities.

After you have categorized and ranked your priorities, it's time to create a mission statement that allows you to pursue goals in each of those three categories. At this point you may be tempted to focus only on the Now, thinking that's enough to deal with. But because of the evolutionary nature of each financial category, your Future and Far Future priorities should be as much a concern in the present as they will be later. Now is the time to prepare for tomorrow's needs.

Review your financial goals on page 109. Now write a financial mission statement that encompasses those goals for each era of your life.

The Now (0–10 years):

The Future (10+ years):

The Far Future (your legacy):

Josh knew his goal had to be attainable; he didn't want to create further frustrations for him and his wife by creating an impossible goal. He also wanted the statement to have a deadline so that he and his wife would stay on course. Josh's mission statement for the Now was:

I will start giving back to God, beginning at 5 percent of my gross pay and increasing the percentage until I reach 10 percent; pay off my credit cards in 18 months; find a way within the next year to budget a life-insurance policy; and create an emergency savings fund of three months' pay within 24 months.

Remain flexible. If you find yourself achieving your goals before the allotted time, tackle the next priority on your list.

Of course, unexpected financial problems happen. This is another reason to keep your statement flexible. If a financial crisis arises, don't give up. Adjust your statement to the situation, but keep going.

Remember, it all comes back to stewardship. God is the owner; you are the manager. It doesn't matter whether you have a few cents or a million dollars—none of us deserve what we have. Everything we have is a gift, and we are the stewards of it. As you take the next step toward financial simplicity, use your mission statement to demonstrate that you are obedient as God's steward and to guide you toward your goal. When you want to give up, remember that you have an incredible God who wants you to succeed, who wants to see you get out of whatever mess you may be in. After all, it's His money; and He wants a good return.

Movement

For many of us our financial situation is less than ideal. OK, for some of us it stinks. The bills have begun to stack up. The income we were expecting at this stage of life has not materialized. Some are trying to fund a lifestyle that doesn't fit with our paycheck.

Many of those in our study were perplexed about how they got in this financial mess. That lack of awareness is the first barrier that prevents movement toward fiscal simplicity. Past decisions litter the pathway. They block us from moving forward, from making our mission statement become more than just goals. The removal of these barriers will get us back to being wise caretakers.

simplelife   STATISTICS ■

50% *say they have more bills than money each month.*
46% *agree their credit-card debt is too high.*
72% *don't have the equivalent of six months' living expenses saved in case of an emergency.*

In the box of statistics on this page, underline any problems you can identify with.

The obstacles need to be removed. Let's take the next step to achieving our financial goals.

■ Understanding Your Barriers

In Acts there is a pretty intense story about a husband, his wife, and their offering. It had not been long since Jesus had left earth, and the church was in its infancy. Acts 2:44 says, "All the believers were together and had everything in common." The body of Christ, the church, was beginning to take shape, and it was becoming something beautiful.

> Read Acts 5:1-11. Why do you think Ananias and Sapphira lied about their gift? Check all that apply.
>
> ☐ They wanted to be seen as supersacrificial.
> ☐ They wanted special standing in the eyes of the church.
> ☐ They wanted their fair share of the sale and didn't want to let go of what they had committed to God.
> ☐ Other:
>
> Why do you think God's judgment was so severe?

The couple's gift itself was good, but the deception ruined it in the eyes of God. In a similar but not nearly as dramatic way, many of our financial struggles are the result of some outside factor, something more personal than many of us would like to admit. It would be easy to say our credit-card balance is the barrier that needs to be eliminated to achieve a simple financial structure, but rarely is that the cause. The debt is the outcome of a barrier, not the barrier itself.

Let's hear from Erin to illustrate: "Look, I know my budget is strained. Trust me, I realize this every time I open the mailbox and see a bill. I get a little nervous, hoping I will have enough to pay for it."

It doesn't take a financial expert to realize that Erin is in a very serious situation. One misstep, and she's in trouble: "I guess I could try to trade in my car for one with a lower monthly payment; but once you have a car like mine, it's hard to take a step down. Everyone loves it; I get so many compliments. I don't know; I guess it just makes me feel good. I feel like I'm somebody when I drive around in it. I don't know if I want to let that go."

Identify Erin's barrier.

☐ Desire to be admired
☐ Car payment
☐ Mounting bills

Did you catch Erin's barrier that has caused her financial strain? It's not the bills. It's not the car. It's deeper than that. Her problem isn't her financial state; that's only where it has manifested itself. Her struggle is with her identity.

We want to point the finger at someone or something else, such as the credit-card companies; but they didn't put the original balance on that card or purchase more than we could afford to pay off. Many times our financial situations arise from our self-identity. This type of barrier causes us to make decisions that are fiscally irresponsible.

We must also be careful when we use our lack of financial resources, also known as our paycheck, as an excuse for our burdens. A lack of money may limit us, but acquiring additional funds does not necessarily mean our financial burdens will be resolved. Often, our monetary problems have nothing to do with money. And even if we got a raise or inherited a bundle, the issues still exist inside us that would give us the same problems on a much grander scale.

Have you ever bought anything to boost your image?
☐ Yes   ☐ No

Was this a one-time thing or part of your lifestyle?

No matter how much money we make, we must first uncover our motivations for our financial decisions before we can become responsible stewards of our resources.

■ Moving Your Motivation

What motivates your financial decisions? One reason the Bible discusses money is that it is such a telling indicator of what's going on inside us. Our monetary decisions flow from our hearts. Jesus said, "Where your treasure is, there your heart will be also" (Matt. 6:21).

A cliché says if you want to look at someone's priorities, just take a look at their checkbook. And there is truth behind this. Recorded in the register are the places or persons we deem important enough to rate a portion of our financial resources.

Examine your checkbook or credit-card statement. Estimate the percentage of money you are spending on the following in an average month.

Food and clothing	____%
Housing	____%
Utilities	____%
Entertainment	____%
Stuff	____%
Education	____%
Church, ministry, missions	____%
Other: _____	____%
_____	____%

When we truthfully answer the question of why we are spending, we come face-to-face with our heart. We see our motivations for what they really are, not as we pretend them to be.

Is debt a problem? Absolutely. Is debt the cause of our financial problems? No.

When we dig deep to the root cause of debt, we often find a common obstacle. Debt is primarily caused by overconsumption. Overconsumption is caused by a desire to have something that is beyond our financial reach. We want something beyond our financial means because we think somehow it will make us more complete.

We are immersed in a culture that teaches consumption as a way of life. We think our purchasing habits, our ways of entangling ourselves with debt, are normal. Satan is great at molding our minds to fit his purposes. If he can get us to justify the one purchase we can't afford, he knows the next will come much more easily. And the results are often frustration and stress, which complicate our lives and ultimately our relationship with God.

If debt is a problem for you, what are the primary causes? Check all that apply.

☐ Overspending/consumption
☐ Inadequate income
☐ Lack of discipline
☐ Lack of clarity about financial goals
☐ Other:

We know it isn't just debt that hinders financial simplicity. There is typically much more. If our answer to the final "Why?" falls short of being acceptable to God, then we must fervently seek to remove that obstacle.

But don't leave it up to your own wisdom. Seek help from the Maker of all things. The "why?" is not hidden from Him. He already knows your struggle; He has seen your heart's true motivation. And most importantly, He understands (see Heb. 4:15-16).

Dig deep for answers. And then present them to the God who came to this tiny rock of a planet to better understand what you are experiencing. With Him, move your motivation.

■ The Far Future, the Future, and the Now

As we discussed yesterday, each one of these eras in your life is separate but highly dependent on the others. Each category holds its own obstacles that, unless removed, limit your movement toward your desired destination.

Movement: The Far Future. Proverbs 13:22 says,

> A good man leaves an inheritance to his grandchildren,
>   but the sinner's wealth is stored up for the righteous.

We should make financial decisions not because they will improve our situation but because they will benefit someone else. This idea swims completely upstream against the suggestion that because we worked hard for it all, we deserve to enjoy it all.

Is there anything wrong with enjoying the fruit of our labor? Absolutely not. But the Bible indicates that there is something wrong when we hoard the fruit of our labor. Why? Because it isn't ours to hoard. There is more beyond our earthly lives, and our death provides one final opportunity to show our love for others.

It is not just our grandchildren for whom we need to be concerned. We also need to be concerned about the future financial security of those we live with now. Too many people don't carry enough insurance to care for their loved ones.

Review your mission statement for the Far Future on page 111. What barriers are keeping you from caring for those who will outlive you?

☐ Preoccupation with yourself
☐ Assuming a tragedy will never occur
☐ Thinking you have plenty of time
☐ Lack of resources
☐ Other:

Sadly, many are left without provision because we didn't place enough importance on those we will leave behind. We need to remove the barriers that hinder our movement to a lasting financial legacy.

simplelife   STATISTICS ■

41% *of males don't have enough insurance.*
51% *of females don't have enough insurance.*
73% *have concerns about whether they will retire comfortably.*

Movement: The Future. God watches over each of us and cares for us more deeply than any of us will ever understand while on this earth. Nevertheless, He allows His followers to make mistakes and to suffer the consequences of those mistakes. For those who do not plan properly for retirement, the results will probably align with the lack of preparation. Most people in our surveys doubt they can retire comfortably, so we heard cries of distress, fear, and discomfort about what the future will bring.

We are a culture that spends first and saves if we have anything left. We splurge in the present at the risk of the future. Without sufficient income we are no longer able to support the lifestyle we once had. We rely on Social Security to get us from one month to the next.

The future is not always about retirement. It's about saving for your child's education. It can be about preparing for the house you've wanted. It's about whatever may come into your financial path beyond the next 10 years.

Examine your mission statement for the Future on page 110. What is your primary goal for the future?

☐ Saving for retirement   ☐ Saving for children's education
☐ Saving for a new home   ☐ Other:

Check any barriers to your goals.

☐ Lack of concern
☐ Living for the present
☐ Lack of resources
☐ Other:

When we don't prepare and the Future becomes the Now, we are left in despair, wondering where the time went and what we could have done differently.

Movement: The Now. Many of us want to set aside something for retirement and the next generation, but we can't see beyond our present financial needs. It's time to figure out what's important and what's not in our financial world. What we do here will either hinder or help this part of our life's journey.

Check the statement that best describes your Now.

☐ I have not yet made a poor financial decision.
☐ I have made some financial mistakes but have been able to recover.
☐ I have made financial mistakes that are still causing problems.
☐ I have managed well financially but need to set clearer goals for the future.
☐ Other:

Wherever you find yourself, good things can come from your finances when you dedicate them to God and commit to be a steward of His resources.

Most financial obstacles are in the present, impacting our day-to-day living, and are therefore powerfully destructive. Satan knows if he can get us to build constrictive blockages to our financial well-being in the present, we will potentially be affected for the rest of our lives.

Examine your mission statement for the Now on page 110. What barriers are in the way?

Barriers to simplicity in the Now may mean a radical change of lifestyle. But if we are honest, our concern with image and fashion is probably not only causing financial disruption but also interfering with our relationship with God. And no designer product is worth that cost.

■ Making the Move

Remember Josh? He wrote this mission statement for his Now:

I will start giving back to God, beginning at 5 percent of my gross pay and increasing the percentage until I reach 10 percent; pay off my credit cards in 18 months; find a way within the next year to budget a life-insurance policy; and create an emergency savings fund of three months' pay within 24 months.

Josh looked back at his list of priorities in each of the three categories—the Now, the Future, and the Far Future—and identified several barriers that were preventing him from moving toward his goals. He decided to select one barrier from each category that he would prayerfully submit to God for help. They were:

- The Now: materialism
- The Future: complacency
- The Far Future: an overt focus on self

Josh looked at what he had written and shook his head. He realized money was not the issue. *He* was the issue.

As we follow Josh's lead to identify our barriers to movement, many of us will find ourselves facing some difficult realities about the state of our hearts. Remember, these obstacles not only hinder our financial simplicity but also hurt our development as Christians. Removing these obstructions will help us reach our financial goals and allow us to take another step closer to becoming more like Jesus.

Look back at the barriers you identified today for each era of your life (activities on pp. 117, 119, and 120). Choose one barrier for each that you will focus on.

The Now:

The Future:

The Far Future:

Spend time in prayer about these barriers. Ask for God's direction as you submit your goals, priorities, and decisions to Him.

Alignment
Day 4 The Uniqueness of You

Our mission statement provides the core around which we line up everything in our lives to support our financial goals. Many times we may find ourselves, having made our purpose clear and having removed many obstacles, still feeling a little out of sync. We have our core, but all that surrounds it doesn't support our goals. We need to make sure our financial activities align with our mission statement. Today we will identify ways to do that.

Honest Assessment

When assessing our ability to align activities with our financial goals, we must be honest with ourselves. A skewed assessment will inhibit our ability to accomplish our mission.

We all have preferences about the way we want others to perceive us. Some go to great lengths to maintain a façade of prosperity, living a lifestyle they can't afford. And of course, an honest assessment is not just about an honest exterior, the one the world sees. Even more important is the interior reality. Have you ever convinced yourself of something you knew was not true? It happens when you want something so badly that you are willing to compromise your own intelligence and reality to avoid a truth you don't want to recognize. As we assess our financial realities, we must be brutally honest.

Assess your alignment by answering the following questions for each era.

The Now

What was my goal?

What changes have I made to meet my goal?

Am I seeing progress?   ☐ Yes   ☐ No

If not, what adjustment needs to take place?

The Future

What was my goal?

What changes have I made to meet my goal?

Am I seeing progress?   ☐ Yes   ☐ No

If not, what adjustment needs to take place?

The Far Future

What was my goal?

What changes have I made to meet my goal?

Am I seeing progress?   ☐ Yes   ☐ No

If not, what adjustment needs to take place?

This honest assessment is an integral part of our stewardship. It is how we can personally hold ourselves accountable for our actions.

> Examine the statistics in the box on this page. In what condition is your debt?

> How healthy is your savings account?

> What have you done to cover you and your family in case of disaster?

simplelife   STATISTICS ■

55% *feel they have too much debt.*
72% *admit they don't have six months' worth of expenses set aside.*
25% *of males say they have enough homeowners' insurance.*
36% *of females say they have enough homeowners' insurance.*

■ Accountability

In Luke 12 Jesus was surrounded by a crowd when someone asked Him, "Teacher, tell my brother to divide the inheritance with me" (v. 13). What a disappointing request. This man came face-to-face with the Creator of the universe, and he could focus only on himself.

> Read Luke 12:13-21. Write a statement Jesus made that summarizes the point of His parable.

The parable itself is extremely appropriate for a discussion of finances. However, the action of this man brings us to the topic of accountability. Like him, we are often blind to what is most important. When it comes to money, it is easy to get distracted by activities that do not align with our mission statement and do not help us realize our goals. We ask the wrong questions. We ignore the opportunity at hand.

We wonder how we can afford a new bedroom suite when we should be figuring out how to have six months of living expenses saved for an emergency. We get distracted by that showroom shine of a new car when we should focus on getting rid of our credit-card debt. So many of our financial decisions don't align with our mission statement. We quickly find out that we cannot do this on our own. We need some type of accountability.

Proper accountability with another person will help you stay on track, encourage you to take off the blinders, and provide incentive to reach your goals. Here are some basic recommendations for seeking someone to hold you accountable for your finances.

- They must have similar values.
- They must understand your financial goals or have similar goals for themselves.
- They must understand money, at least on a basic level.
- They must be trustworthy.
- They must be willing to provide honest feedback.
- They cannot be a family member.

Whom would you trust to help you stay accountable in your finances?

How would you establish that accountability?

▪ Priorities and Personalities

The methods of managing money vary widely. Stephanie likes her financial records to be electronic. Mr. Graham gets freaked out if paper is not involved. Larry does everything over the phone. Ms. Tishner would be lost without her debit card.

We all have our preferred methods of handling our finances. While we are trying to simplify our finances, we will inevitably run across ideas that go against our nature. Because God has given us different gifts and personalities, it makes sense to find ways of managing our finances that help us reach our goals with greater ease.

Herman didn't like details. He wanted to reduce his monthly spending, but all of the number crunching just got annoying. Instead of giving up, he tried to find an approach that would not only meet his goal but also better match his personality. After doing some investigation, Herman found out that his bank had options that allowed him to keep track of his spending without having to concentrate too much on those tedious calculations.

Herman made an important realization: the means by which he was attempting to rein in his spending was not aligned with his personality. This made the process of simplification a burden on his life. And even though the activity itself was aligned, there were better options for Herman. Fortunately, he was able to discover ways that better lined up with who God created him to be.

Does your financial plan match your gifts and personality? If you are not a detail person, a detailed budget may drive you crazy. If you have trouble disciplining yourself to tithe or save, you may need a plan that does it automatically for you.

Identify any current ways of managing that don't fit who you are.

If you feel that your actions are not you, you're probably right. There are numerous ways you can handle your money. Find those that align with who you were meant to be.

■ Willingness to Adjust

As we travel life's journey, our financial situation inevitably changes. There will be highs and lows, valleys and peaks. External factors such as income increases and decreases, financial emergencies, and the birth of a child will impact your situation.

Simplicity requires flexibility. Activities to which we have become accustomed may no longer be the best route. Change could happen in a week, month, or year. Be prepared. Be flexible.

Identify any recent, significant life changes.

How do your financial strategies need to change in response to these events?

■ The Acceptance of Imperfection

We find our friend, Josh, back at the coffee shop talking with a friend. He had set up a time when he and Lucas could get together biweekly to talk about progress with his finances. It had been a crucial step to be accountable to someone other than his wife.

"So tell me about God's 10 percent," asked Lucas.

This had been an issue for Josh. It was the first goal of his mission statement for the Now (p. 120). Josh had taken action in every step except giving back to God, so he and Lucas discussed how Josh could create an activity that would align with this goal. They determined it would be best if Josh gave his company permission to directly deposit a portion of his paycheck into a savings account, opened for the specific purpose of setting aside money for God. This way God's money would come out of his paycheck first, eliminating the temptation to use it for other purposes.

Circle the step Josh struggled with.

Clarity   Movement   Alignment   Focus

Even though Josh had the desire to meet his goal, he had an alignment issue. By reevaluating his alignment, he figured out a way to adjust his actions to meet not only the first but also his other desires. Like Josh, you will find areas in your life that do not match your desired outcome. If you need to adjust, that's OK. Remember, this is a process. Approach errors as an opportunity to learn, grow, and further define who you yearn to be. Don't strive for perfection. Strive for the goal.

Identify the part of each mission statement with which it will be most difficult for you to align your actions.

Now:

Future:

Far Future:

Are you willing to accept your imperfections and start afresh when you don't stick with the financial plan established by your mission statement?   ☐ Yes   ☐ No

Pray about your alignment. Write ways God has shown that your activities need to align more closely with your financial goals, as expressed in your mission statements on pages 110–11.

Focus

Today you will make some difficult decisions in regard to your finances. By this point you've probably made a lot of great decisions and followed through with action. But you realize there is more. There are some weights that still burden your progress. Choosing to get out of debt was easy. Finding yourself in a place where it is either your child's cheerleading trip or a notable decrease in that debt can be gut-wrenching. Deciding where to place your attention requires focus.

■ A Briefing on Focus

Focus is a willingness to eliminate even good things that don't contribute to the overall pursuit of our goals, at least for the time being. Following are some characteristics of financial focus for the simple life.

Focus sees the whole picture. All financial decisions are connected; one impacts the other. For every dollar you spend on gas, you have one less dollar to spend, save, or invest somewhere else. No financial decisions stand alone or disconnected. Focus requires us to see this big picture—the fact that everything is intertwined, for better or worse.

Recall Josh's dilemma. His family was in debt, but his daughter wanted to go on a cheerleading trip. Josh must consider the fact that debt had and would continue to have a direct impact on his entire family. He had to consider the stress and the shifty ground on which his family's finances sat. Was it more important to create a solid surface on which he and his family could continue to build for many years, or was it more important to send his daughter on a cheerleading trip? Would it benefit his daughter more to have a family with solid finances, or would it benefit her more to learn how to develop new cheerleading skills? This was more than a trip. It was a piece of the family's financial picture. And whatever the decision would be, the total picture would be affected.

> Identify a financial decision you have made that affected your total financial picture.

Focus is blind to the externals. In horse racing, blinders are placed on the sides of a horse's eyes so that its vision is limited to only what is in front of him. In a race there are several horses on the track; most are running within inches of other competitors. If the horse is distracted by the others next to it, it might slow down and lose the race.

In our financial lives, a lot of things are going on around us, and distraction comes easily. Strapping on a pair of financial blinders can help us reach the final goal. As we proceed on this journey, we must be willing to look ahead and allow the externals to fade away.

No competitor enters a race without the intent to reach the finish line. As a horse dashes around the track with a single goal, you must continue this race and be purposeful about crossing the finish line—reaching your financial goal.

> Review your financial mission statements on pages 110–11. What issues are currently distracting you from your long-term financial goals?

Focus distinguishes between the good and the best. As you work on the goals outlined in your financial mission statements, you may find yourself in a situation where you must distinguish between a necessary good and an unnecessary good. Our finances can provide us with the opportunity to do many great things. We can feed the hungry, give to the poor, and take care of our family.

But sometimes the good can limit us in our pursuit of simplicity. God wants us to take care of others, but rarely does He ask us to put ourselves in financial ruin and become another's burden. We can give until it hurts, but then we find ourselves hurt.

You have already determined what is important in your finances. Anything above and beyond needs to be prayerfully questioned until you are on solid financial ground. Make sure the good is not preventing you from achieving the best.

List expenses that are good but not absolutely necessary. Think about the money you spend on expensive cups of coffee, snacks, clothes, a nice car, electronics, and so forth. Also record the amount of money you spend on these things in a year.

Good but Not Necessary Expenses	Amount per Year
	$_____
	$_____
	$_____
	$_____
	$_____
	$_____
	$_____
	$_____
	$_____
	$_____
	$_____
	$_____
	$_____

Go back and check the items you will eliminate to provide resources for better causes.

■ Focus on the Now, Future, and Far Future

Focus on the Now (0–10 years). Our surveys showed that the respondents desired a better lifestyle for their children than they had experienced as children. Desiring to care for our children isn't a bad motive. We want them to wear the best, drive the best, and experience the best. But at what cost? For those who can't afford to do so, this desire to provide materially beyond the children's needs is a barrier that hinders the family from simplifying their finances. What can be a good desire can turn into a money pit.

Review your mission statement for the Now (p. 110) and decide what you can eliminate to reach your goal.

simplelife   STATISTICS ■

77% *of men say they want to give their children more materially than they had growing up.*

68% *of women say they want to give their children more materially than they had growing up.*

50% *want to give their children more than they have already given them.*

50% *don't have financial plans for the future.*

73% *have concerns about whether they can comfortably retire.*

41% *of males believe they don't have enough insurance.*

51% *of females believe they don't have enough insurance.*

Focus on the Future (10+ years). It's simple: we need to set aside money for the future. Because money is finite, we have to make hard decisions about spending in the present.

Maybe you determined that your retirement is your greatest need, but you also need to start saving for your son's college expenses. Your mission statement reflects the next step in your retirement planning, and your funds are limited. This is why you created a mission statement. You need to reflect on your statement and let it guide your focus. Maybe you can help with college at a later date. Maybe your son can start saving some for himself.

Identify an area of your mission statement for your Future (p. 110) that requires you to save more money. What do you need to change to get on track with your savings plan?

Focus on the Far Future (your legacy). Trent wanted to make sure that, even after his death, his wife and two children had enough. He also wanted to leave insurance money to his church. Trent looked at his financial situation. There was no way he could do both. The premium on both of those insurance policies would squeeze his available funds. Trent knew he and his wife had created a mission statement that addressed the insurance need for his family. Focus required that Trent make priorities. His family was his priority.

The lack of insurance is a reality that many face. There are many reasons to have insurance, including legacy building. As you pursue your legacy, don't stretch yourself too thin. Focus on the mission statement and allow it to govern the direction of your legacy. As time progresses, you will be able to build your legacy and thereby bless future generations.

Review your mission statement for the Far Future (p. 111).
Check anything you need to do to bring focus to your Far Future.

☐ Give more to your church and other Kingdom causes
☐ Save more for retirement
☐ Save more to leave a legacy for those you love
☐ Eliminate expenses in order to save
☐ Other:

■ What Focus Must Not Eliminate

We are stewards of God's resources. It's His money, not ours. Yet He asks us to give back to Him a portion of what He gives us (see Deut. 12:6; Mal. 3:10). The act of offering our money to God has two purposes:

1. To participate in God's work
2. To reveal our hearts

God doesn't need our money. He created the concept of giving so that we can be obedient to Him. He wants us to live beyond what is humanly possible, to tap into spiritual blessings. Giving was fashioned from God's love for us.

In 2 Corinthians 8:3-4 the apostle Paul wrote about a Macedonian church that understood its need to participate in God's plan: "I testify that, on their own, according to their ability and beyond their ability, they begged us insistently for the privilege of sharing in the ministry to the saints." The people of this church wanted to be a part of something beyond themselves. They begged to participate in God's work through their gifts. They were created for all the good that God originally designed, including the spiritually fulfilling act of giving.

In the same letter Paul wrote about the connection between a person's heart and his offering: "Each person should do as he has decided in his heart—not out of regret or out of necessity, for God loves a cheerful giver" (2 Cor. 9:7). Many Christians argue that we need to give 10 percent of our earnings to the church, based on texts from Malachi 3 and 1 Corinthians 16. But what are we to make of the previous verse?

A good way to answer this question is to take a look at the Ten Commandments. When God presented these commands to the Israelites, He set the bar pretty low. Do not kill. Do not have sex with someone other than you spouse. The basics.

But then came additional teachings from Jesus. He did not make these commandments optional but taught that there was so much more. Everything, including these basics, was about the heart. And when the heart is involved, a change occurs.

Now anger at your brother is on the same level as murder.

Now adultery includes lust.

God wants more from you than a mind full of do's and don'ts. He wants your heart.

The same goes for Scriptures on giving. Offering a tenth of your earnings is basic. Supporting the ministry of your local church is the low bar. When God starts to look at the heart, the bar bumps up. We no longer offer only what Scripture says is appropriate but what the Holy Spirit instructs us to give. It is a gift known only by you and God.

Read Jesus' response to a widow's offering:

"Summoning His disciples, He said to them, 'I assure you: This poor widow has put in more than all those giving to the temple treasury. For they all gave out of their surplus, but she out of her poverty has put in everything she possessed—all she had to live on' " (Mark 12:43-44).

Why was Jesus impressed with the woman's gift? Check one.

☐ She gave sacrificially from the heart.
☐ She gave more than anyone else.
☐ She always gave a lot of money.

No rich offering could match the heart of this widow. Her gift, the gift of her heart, was worth more than any bag of money.

Withholding your offering is dismissing an invitation to participate in God's work. This is one area that should not be eliminated by focus. To miss out on giving is to miss out on one of the beautiful acts of obedience that God provides for us.

Giving is a gift created for you. Immerse yourself in the experience. Pray for God to direct your heart in giving your offerings. Be a part of something beyond your human capability.

Check the statements that are true of you.

☐ I am giving a tithe to God's work.
☐ I give beyond the tithe as I am able.
☐ I give cheerfully from the heart.
☐ I give sacrificially.
☐ I give reluctantly.
☐ I would like to give more but am not financially able.

Pray about your giving patterns and your heart. What changes is God directing you to make in order to bring focus to this area of stewardship?

You have clarified, moved, aligned, and focused in the area of finances. This is not the end but a beginning. It is time to create a new standard for handling money. It is time to shift your view of the role finances can play during your lifetime.

Stewardship is an awesome responsibility and opportunity. When God requests stewardship, He hands us a gift that allows us to develop spiritually and to make a positive difference. Take the gift. Tear the wrapping. Open the box. Explore the contents. Experience how stewardship can make a difference for now and eternity.

How to Get Closer to God

■ SESSION 5
Group Experience

1. Bills, credit-card debt, or inadequate savings—which one of these is your primary financial challenge?
2. Christian money management is rooted in the biblical concept of stewardship. Define *stewardship*.
3. What does it mean to be a caretaker of God's resources?

Clarity

1. How can money or possessions distort a person's priorities?
2. Share the financial mission statements you wrote for the three stages of life (pp. 110–11): Now (0–10 years), Future (10+ years), and Far Future (legacy).

Movement

1. What are some of the issues behind many people's spending habits?
2. Read Matthew 6:21. What do your spending patterns reveal about the priorities in your life?
3. Discuss barriers to your goals for the three stages of life.

Alignment

1. With which financial goals will it be most difficult to align your actions?
2. Share your reaction to the idea of enlisting someone to hold you accountable for your financial management.
3. Share the method you use to manage your money.
4. Name some life changes that require adjustments to your family's financial plan.

Focus

1. Identify decisions that can impact your whole financial picture.
2. What tends to distract you from your financial goals?
3. Name expenses that aren't necessary to your financial goals.
4. Share things you have committed to eliminate to reach your financial goals for the Now, the Future, and the Far Future.
5. Why is giving to God an important part of your financial plan?

Looking for God

1. Show the DVD for session 5. Complete the viewer guide below.

How to Get Closer to God

Results of Acts 6:4

The preaching ministry grew more _____.
More people became _____ of Christ.
Some of the hardest to reach became _____.

Your Relationship with God

Deal realistically with your _____ world.
Be brutally _____ with yourself and others.
Be _____ in discovering alternatives.
Acknowledge that something _____ has to go.
Keep your _____.

2. Discuss Jack's story. In what ways can you relate to him?
3. Share prayer requests related to finances. Pray in pairs for these concerns, asking God for wisdom and discipline to make changes.

Complete week 5 devotionals and activities before the next group session.

If you missed this session, go to www.lifeway.com/downloads
to download this or any other session of Simple Life.

simple
life

Jack, 43 years old, is the vice president of a midsize software company. He and Laura, happily married for 17 years, have three sons.

Work consumes Jack's life. We asked him where he would spend more time if he could. He named his wife and his sons and then added, "But if I had to pick just one area where I would spend more time, it would be with God."

Jack was raised in a Christian home, and he and Laura are members of a nondenominational church today. "Yeah, we are members. But I bet the other members wouldn't recognize me if I showed up next Sunday. I haven't been to church in more than six months, and I have taken the family only three times in the past two years.

Jack's faith and his church were formative in his life. He even admits they were his most important influences. Yet despite his background and beliefs, for all practical purposes Jack has left the church. He continued, "Sometimes I get so frustrated with my schedule and so filled with guilt about my neglect of spiritual matters that I cry out to God and ask Him where He is. I feel guilty watching my three sons grow up without church being a part of their lives. I keep asking God for help, but I guess I just need to slow down and listen to Him. I know I'm looking for God in all the wrong places."

What do you think has caused Jack to drift away from God? Have you remained connected to God through the years, or have you also drifted away from Him?

The fourth area of focus in the simple life is your relationship with God. Like Jack, you can be very successful in life but miss out on what's most important. Or you can take steps now to place God at the center of your life and let Him bring your priorities into focus.

Clarity

■ **Day 1** God at the Center

The Bible teaches us, "The fool says in his heart, 'God does not exist' " (Ps. 14:1). Apparently, most of those we surveyed agreed. You can see from the statistics on this page that most said they were Christians. Only 2 percent were either agnostics (persons who claim neither faith nor disbelief in God) or atheists (persons who deny that God exists).

simplelife   STATISTICS ■

80% *say they are Christians.*
 7% *hold to some other religious belief.*
11% *believe in God but have no preferred religious system.*
 2% *are agnostics or atheists.*
69% *say they need to spend more time on spiritual matters.*
90% *feel it's important for them and their families to have
          a spiritual foundation.*
80% *agree it's important to live by biblical values.*
80% *try to provide good spiritual leadership in their families.*

How do Americans feel about their relationships with God? Most respondents said they need to spend more time on spiritual matters.

A large majority surveyed also felt it is important for them and their families to have a spiritual foundation and to live by biblical values. And the majority indicated they try to provide good spiritual leadership in their families. Yet most of these same people said they aren't making enough room in their lives for God.

In short, there is a big discrepancy in these people's lives between desire and reality. Between knowing what is right and following through with action. Between saying that God is their priority and making Him their priority.

Most respondents said their priorities are mixed up and messed up. Most of them realized they need a simpler life that puts God in his rightful place—at the center of their lives. So it's time for a change. Clarity is the first step in doing that.

Do you feel that you need to spend more time with God?
☐ Yes ☐ No

If so, what is preventing you?

Recall Jack's story on page 140. He knew he wanted to put God back at the center of his life. He knew he needed to provide spiritual leadership for his wife and three sons. He made his intentions specific in this mission statement:

I plan to put God back into my life. I will start with some modest goals like reading my Bible 15 minutes a day, taking my family to church on Sunday, and talking about spiritual matters with my family at least once a week.

Notice that Jack's statement included three simple actions he was willing to take:

1. Reading his Bible daily
2. Taking his family to church on Sunday
3. Talking about spiritual matters with his family

Of course, growing closer to God isn't a magic formula. It's possible to read the Bible, go to church, and talk about spiritual matters and still not have God at the center of your life.

When Jesus walked this earth as a man, He recognized that someone could have all the outward manifestations of spirituality and still be distant from God. In fact, He often encountered such a group of people. They were called Pharisees.

The name *Pharisee* means *separated ones*. There were probably a few thousand Pharisees in Jesus' time. These guys refrained from any defilement and rigorously kept the Old Testament laws. The Pharisees added other traditions to ensure their obedience to the law. They had dietary rituals. They had rituals of purity at meals. To keep the Sabbath holy, they had a set of rules for the work that could be done on the Sabbath.

The strict traditions of the Pharisees caused some of them to be legalistic. Instead of emphasizing internal change, they externalized God's law. They relied on different types of external obedience in their attempts to get closer to God.

These guys didn't make Jesus happy. On the contrary, He was disgusted with them. Just listen to an excerpt of His denunciation of the Pharisees: "Woe to you, scribes and Pharisees, hypocrites! You are like whitewashed tombs, which appear beautiful on the outside, but inside are full of dead men's bones and every impurity. In the same way, on the outside you seem righteous to people, but inside you are full of hypocrisy and lawlessness" (Matt. 23:27-28).

Why did Jesus accuse the Pharisees of being hypocrites?

A checklist of good works doesn't bring someone closer to God unless those actions come from the heart of someone who truly desires to put God at the center of his or her life. In fact, if we have a desire to get closer to God, and we have no actions that move us in that direction, we are probably not getting closer to God. The Bible clearly says, "Faith, if it doesn't have works, is dead by itself" (Jas. 2:17).

Sixty-nine percent of those we surveyed indicated they really wanted to move closer to God. But desire without specificity typically leads nowhere. So we aren't proposing that you just have outward manifestations of religion like the Pharisees. Instead, we are proposing that you plan concrete actions that will demonstrate your inner desire for a close walk with God. Writing a mission statement will help you do that.

Before writing your mission statement, indicate some actions you are already taking to get closer to God.

☐ Have a regular prayer time
☐ Regularly read and/or study the Bible
☐ Memorize Scripture
☐ Fast
☐ Faithfully attend church
☐ Minister to others in Jesus' name
☐ Share your faith
☐ Other:

You don't get closer to God just by going through a checklist of items. But you may need to take actions to move closer to God because little or nothing is happening in your life to help you grow spiritually.

As you think about what to include in your mission statement, remember these points.

- You must have a desire to grow closer to God. If you see this exercise as a legalistic checklist, you have completely missed the point. Write only what you know in your heart you need and want to do.

- You must be intentional about following this mission statement. It can't be just an idea or a concept. It must be a plan or a process for making progress. Then ask God to help you carry it out. "I plan to show love to God" is not a mission statement. "I plan to show love to God by spending 30 minutes a day in prayer" includes a plan.
- The statement should be a starting point. Your goals should be realistic and attainable.

Write your mission statement for developing a closer relationship with God.

In our surveys we heard from hundreds of people that they wanted a simple life closer to God. And they had specific ideas about what that meant. Tomorrow we will discuss the three biggest steps they wanted to take.

Clarity

Those who completed our surveys indicated that a closer relationship with God included three important elements: the church, the Bible, and open discussion of their faith.

■ The Simple Life and the Local Church

The local church gets its share of criticism these days. And we Christians often deserve the reviews we get. The church is full of hypocrites. The church has its problems and sometimes presents a bad story to the watching world.

The church of two thousand years ago also had problems. In the church in Jerusalem, people complained that their ministry needs were being ignored. The church at Corinth dealt with terrible infighting, immorality, and the abuse of spiritual gifts. The churches in Galatia struggled with doctrinal issues. Even in the joyous fellowship at Philippi, a curious battle took place between two women in the church.

These are only a few of the not-so-pleasant stories we learn about the churches of the New Testament. But we still hunger for the fellowship of God's people.

Read Hebrews 10:24-25:

"Let us be concerned about one another in order to promote love and good works, not staying away from our meetings, as some habitually do, but encouraging each other, and all the more as you see the day drawing near" (Heb. 10:24-25).

Why do we hunger for church fellowship?

No one claims the church is perfect. But still God's people come together to encourage one another, worship God together, love one another, and do good works together.

Many of those with whom we spoke don't attend church regularly, but they admit something is missing from their lives. They seem to understand the need for Christian fellowship. They seem to know that in order to get closer to God, they need to be around others who worship Him.

simplelife   STATISTICS ■

29% *attend church weekly.*
51% *of born-again Christians attend church weekly.*
75% *of evangelicals attend church weekly.*

Do you regularly attend church?   ☐ Yes   ☐ No

How does your church help you grow in your relationship with God?

We also learned that those who don't attend church are not antichurch and don't harbor resentment toward Christians in the church. But when these unchurched people decide to visit a church, they often have to summon great courage to walk into a place where they know few, if any, people. And they often tell us they feel excluded and on the outside ("not part of the club," one person said matter-of-factly).

It looks like a lot of people may be looking to return to church. We hope we Christians don't run them off.

■ The Simple Life and the Bible

The results of our study were fascinating in many ways, but the responses on issues of spirituality were among the most surprising. For example, a whopping 82 percent said the Bible should be their moral compass, their family's guide, and their blueprint for the simple life.

But here's the catch. The vast majority of Americans, including churchgoing Christians, are really ignorant about the Bible. Most of us don't know the Bible. The reason? We don't read the Bible.

simplelife   STATISTICS ■

89% *say it's important to have a spiritual foundation.*

81% *say they need to provide stronger spiritual leadership for their children.*

82% *say they need to live by the values of the Bible.*

Check all that apply.

☐ The Bible is the moral compass for my life.
☐ The Bible is my family's guide for instruction and living.
☐ I study the Bible regularly.
☐ I teach the Bible to my children.

If you couldn't check all four statements, what is causing a disconnect between your priorities and your practices?

■ The Simple Life and Open Discussion of Faith

Most respondents to our surveys said they need to be open about their Christian faith. Six of 10 bluntly said they should openly discuss spiritual matters with others.

So much for keeping your religion to yourself.

simplelife   STATISTICS ■

60% *say they should openly discuss spiritual matters with others.*

Mitchell, a 28-year-old married man from Iowa, expressed the conviction well: "If something really means something to you, you talk about it openly. I am originally from Indianapolis, and I am a diehard Colts fan. You can't get me to shut up about my Colts. So I don't think you can really grow in your faith unless you are open about it. That's what I need to be doing more, especially with my family."

Early in the life of the Jerusalem church, the religious authorities threatened Peter and John and told them to stop speaking about their faith in Christ. Their response was bold and straightforward: "We are unable to stop speaking about what we have seen and heard" (Acts 4:20).

How openly do you talk about your faith?

☐ Never   ☐ Seldom   ☐ Occasionally   ☐ Frequently

The simple life means getting closer to God. That closeness comes when we unashamedly speak about our beliefs.

■ Clarity, God, and the Simple Life

Maybe as you have focused on your relationship with God, you realized something is missing from your life. Perhaps you realized Someone is missing from your life. And you also realized you will never get your life in order until you give priority to the One who created you. Let us share with you how to do that.

The Bible teaches that God revealed Himself to the world through His Son, Jesus Christ. The Bible also makes it clear that people cannot enter the perfection that is God because we have sin in our lives: "All have sinned and fall short of the glory of God" (Rom. 3:23). The imperfect can't be in the presence of God, who is perfect and holy.

Did you catch the word *all?* That's everybody. That's Art and Thom. That's people who seem to have it all together. That's you. None of us are good enough or can do enough good things to get to God. Sin keeps us from Him. That's the bad news.

But the good news is that God provided a way for our sins to be forgiven. He sent His Son, Jesus, into the world to die for us, to take the punishment for our sins. The Bible says it clearly: "He made the One who did not know sin to be sin for us, so that we might become the righteousness of God in Him" (2 Cor. 5:21).

And why did God willingly give His Son to die for us? "God loved the world in this way: He gave His One and Only Son, so that everyone who believes in Him will not perish but have eternal life" (John 3:16).

The beginning point of getting closer to God is to know God through His Son, Jesus Christ. You must first admit that you are a sinner and that you want God to forgive your sins. That turning away from sins is called repentance in the Bible.

To be acceptable to God, you must, by faith, accept what Jesus did for you by dying on the cross. He took the punishment for you. And you must believe that Jesus not only died but also rose from the dead. He conquered death. And when we trust Jesus to be our Savior, He forgives our sins and gives us the promise and hope of eternal life in heaven.

Such is the greatest gift ever offered and given.

If you want to accept Jesus as your Savior, pause and pray. Confess your sin and ask Him to forgive you and give you eternal life through His sacrifice on the cross and His resurrection from the dead.

If you are already a Christian but are not following Jesus as closely as you should be, now is the time to turn back to Him. Pray and ask God to guide you to actions that will help you pursue a closer relationship with Him. Indicate anything He directs you to do.

☐ Have a regular prayer time
☐ Regularly read and/or study the Bible
☐ Memorize Scripture
☐ Fast
☐ Faithfully attend church
☐ Minister to others in Jesus' name
☐ Share your faith
☐ Other:

Now is the time for clarity. That's the first step of the simple life as you seek to follow God more closely.

Examine the mission statement you wrote on page 145. Revise it to include anything God directed you to do in the previous activity. Rewrite your statement here.

We suggest you share your mission statement with someone. Ask them if you can be accountable to them for six months or a year to stay on track in your walk with God. That person needs to be someone with whom you don't mind sharing your struggles and your victories.

I shared my mission statement with

_____

on this date: _____.

Also make yourself accountable to God. Pause now and ask for His strength to complete the goals expressed by your mission statement.

Movement

No one likes traffic congestion. Congestion hinders progress. We need to move in one direction, but congestion stops us or detours us. We can't be our best or do our best when congestion gets in the way.

Do you have congestion in your relationship with God? Our research shows that a significant majority of people admit they need and desire a healthier relationship with God. Most people want a strong spiritual foundation. They want to get closer to God and to spend more time with Him. But nearly 7 of 10 (69 percent) in our study desire more time for church and other spiritual matters. God is not in the picture in many lives. Congestion is in the way.

Jeannie is an artist who lives in Franklin, Tennessee. We asked her what she thought she needed to have a more complete life. Her response was straightforward: "That's easy. I would like to get closer to God."

So, we asked, where do you attend church?

"I don't."

How often do you read the Bible?

"Not much."

Do you pray regularly?

"Nope, sporadically."

A pattern was developing.

"Look," Jeannie told us. "You can ask me questions all day about my spirituality, and I'm not going to fare well. That's what I'm getting at. I'm not close to God, but I want to be. And I really don't have a good excuse. I've just never made a habit of those things I know I should be doing. I'm too busy for my own good. I guess I'm too busy for God."

Read Philippians 3:12:

"Not that I have already reached the goal or am already fully mature, but I make every effort to take hold of it because I also have been taken hold of by Christ Jesus" (Phil. 3:12).

What enabled Paul to move forward on his spiritual journey?

The apostle Paul was determined to get closer to God, but he knew he had not reached his goal. Still he didn't quit. In fact, he was able to move forward because Christ had already done the work. Paul could make every effort because Christ was his strength. Paul reached toward what was ahead. He pursued the goal. He removed the congestion and had clear movement toward God.

Now that you have clarity, a clear goal in mind, let's see what's next in pursuing a closer relationship with God. Movement toward God can be summed in five words: *prayerful, forgetful, incremental, immediate,* and *resilient.*

◼ Movement Toward God: Prayerful

I (Thom) struggle with consistency in my prayer life. I read about great prayer warriors who spent hours in prayer, and I am ashamed. I have trouble focusing for 30 minutes. I begin my conversation with God, but I often start thinking about my to-do list for the day. So I ask God to help me with my prayer life.

Read Philippians 4:6:

"Don't worry about anything, but in everything, through prayer and petition with thanksgiving, let your requests be made known to God" (Phil. 4:6).

How is worry related to prayer?

What does it mean to present everything to God in prayer?

How does thanksgiving relate to prayer?

Paul said in *everything* let your requests be made known to God. He wants you to take all your needs, burdens, worries, and cares to Him in prayer. So your first step in a better prayer life is to pray for a better prayer life.

You've already established clarity for getting closer to God. The next step is action. Clarity must shift to movement. Your goals must also be an action plan. That's where we often fail, isn't it?

We plan to read the Bible, but we don't do it.

And we plan to get closer to God, but we don't do it.

Clarity says to have a good plan. Movement says to act on the plan. And that's often where the breakdown occurs. That's why we begin with prayer. We need to begin with God, not ourselves. We ask for His strength, not our own.

What are some obstacles that keep you from praying as much as you need to?

Pause and pray that God will draw you closer to Him as you practice spiritual disciplines like prayer. Ask Him to help you overcome the obstacles that are keeping you from having a closer relationship with Him.

Stop depending on your limited ability and start depending on the One who has no limits. Nothing moves congestion like prayer.

■ Movement Toward God: Forgetful

Being forgetful is bad, right? Not always. Paul said with confidence, "One thing I do: forgetting what is behind and reaching forward to what is ahead, I pursue as my goal the prize promised by God's heavenly call in Christ Jesus" (Phil. 3:13-14). It's really amazing. The apostle talked about his singular focus in life, and the first thing he mentioned is that he forgot.

You see, forgetting is not always bad. In fact, it can be positively life-changing. You've set goals before and planned to get closer to God, thinking this time it would work. But it didn't. So now you are paralyzed from moving forward because of past failures.

Listen to Stephanie's story.

"I'm a divorcee," she began with her eyes looking downward. "My husband left me three years ago. And he had every right to leave. I had an affair with his best friend. Well, I guess you would say his former best friend. I can't explain myself to this day. I didn't love his friend. I loved my husband. I still love him."

Stephanie responded in our surveys that she wanted to move closer to God. She had begun attending church, regularly reading her Bible, and praying every day. But then she stopped. Why?

"I just feel like such a failure," she admitted. "I don't know if I can ever love or be loved again by anyone, including God."

Jesus met a woman who probably felt a lot like Stephanie.

Read John 8:1-12. How did Jesus deal with the woman's sin?

How did Jesus instruct the woman to deal with her past?

Jesus, the One who is God, forgave the woman's sin and told her to forget about it. Leave it behind. Go and sin no more.

Is it possible that some of the congestion you are experiencing is because you can't forget? Colossians 1:13-14 reminds you that Jesus has redeemed your past: "He has rescued us from the domain of darkness and transferred us into the kingdom of the Son He loves, in whom we have redemption, the forgiveness of sins."

He has forgiven. Now you must forget and move forward.

Look at the mission statement you wrote for a closer relationship with God (p. 151). How are you doing? Have you started and failed?

Read 1 John 1:9:

"If we confess our sins, He is faithful and righteous to forgive us our sins and to cleanse us from all unrighteousness."

Confess your sins and failures in your relationship with God and ask Him to forgive you. Claim His forgiveness and commit to a growing relationship with Him.

■ Movement Toward God: Incremental

You mission statement is also an action plan. Therefore, it has to be realistic. If we set goals that are too ambitious, we will become discouraged and frustrated. Your mission statement is a beginning, not an end. You must move at a pace that is sustainable.

Don't be a Christian meteor. You've seen the type. She starts out really serious about getting closer to God. She spends 15 hours a week at the church. She prays two hours a day. She reads the Bible two hours a day. She goes on three international mission trips in one year. And then she completely burns out.

A relationship with God will take time to develop. Begin with simple, incremental steps. You'll remove a lot of congestion that way. And one year from now, you may be surprised at your progress.

> Examine your mission statement (p. 151) to determine whether the action steps are too large. Identify the first incremental step you will work on in your relationship with God.

■ Movement Toward God: Immediate

Let's return to the story of the adulterous woman. Jesus clearly communicated to her that she was forgiven. But then what did He tell her? "Go, and from now on do not sin anymore" (John 8:11). Notice that Jesus did not say, "Give this serious thought and after a few weeks change your lifestyle." No, he told her to sin no more. Right then. At that very moment. Change your lifestyle without delay.

In our research one of the main sources of congestion was "soon."

- "Soon I will start going to church again."
- "Soon I plan to begin reading my Bible every day."
- "Soon I will start talking about spiritual matters with my family."

Of course, "soon" never happens. It's put on the shelf of good intentions. But "soon" becomes "never." Movement is hindered by congestion, and one of the most common forms of congestion is procrastination.

The writer of Hebrews addressed this issue in an unusual way: "Watch out, brothers, so that there won't be in any of you an evil, unbelieving heart that departs from the living God. But encourage each other daily, while it is still called today, so that none of you is hardened by sin's deception" (Heb. 3:12-13). The writer said to encourage one another "while it is still called today." Daily doesn't mean soon. Daily doesn't mean tomorrow. Daily doesn't mean when you get around to it. Daily means today, now, at this very moment.

What part of your mission statement do you tend to procrastinate on?

What part of your mission statement will you commit to implement immediately?

■ Movement Toward God: Resilient

The apostle Paul provides an example for many aspects of the simple life. Second Corinthians 11:24-28 gives us a glimpse of the trials he endured:

Five times I received from the Jews 40 lashes minus one. Three times I was beaten with rods. Once I was stoned. Three times I was shipwrecked. I have spent a night and a day in the depths of the sea. On frequent journeys, I faced dangers from rivers, dangers from robbers, dangers from my own people, dangers from the Gentiles, dangers in the city, dangers in the open country, dangers on the sea, and dangers among false brothers; labor and hardship, many sleepless nights, hunger and thirst, often without food, cold, and lacking clothing. Not to mention other things, there is the daily pressure on me: my care for all the churches.

Not such a pretty life, was it? But Paul always bounced back. He never gave up.

Read 2 Corinthians 12:10:

"Because of Christ, I am pleased in weaknesses, in insults, in catastrophes, in persecutions, and in pressures. For when I am weak, then I am strong" (2 Cor. 12:10).

Why did Paul never give up in spite of so much hardship?

Paul was truly resilient.

The simple life means we start taking some serious steps toward getting closer to God. Maybe you feel the fear of failure is just too great. In the past you've tried to read the Bible every day, have a daily prayer time, and go to church each week. And you've failed. What's the use of trying yet again?

Movement means we try again. And if we fail, we try again. It means we are resilient and do not give up.

Not too long ago one of the most viewed YouTube videos was "The Last Lecture," featuring Randy Pausch, a professor at Carnegie Mellon University. Pausch, at age 46, was diagnosed with pancreatic cancer. Instead of going into a shell and giving up, he continued to live his life to the fullest. He could have had a pity party about leaving behind a loving wife and three children. He could have said life isn't fair. He could have been angry. He could have given up.

"The Last Lecture" is just that. It is Pausch's final lecture at the university where he served as a professor. It reveals his indomitable spirit and incredible attitude. One of our favorite quotations from Pausch in this final lecture is "I'm dying and I'm having fun. And I'm going to keep having fun every day I have left."[1]

Pausch died on July 25, 2008, at age 47. But he never gave up.

How will resilience help you move toward your goals for growing closer to God?

■ Movement and Getting Closer to God

The pattern of the simple life is clarity, movement, alignment, and focus. The big stumbling block in the simple life is movement. Why? Because movement means we have to change our habits. And by our very nature we are creatures of habit. Movement means you have to break many of your habitual patterns.

Check any habits that keep you from moving closer to God.

☐ Spending too much time on entertainment instead of time with God and His Word

☐ Staying up so late on Saturday night that you can't attend church on Sunday

☐ Spending money on other things, so that none is left for God

☐ Spending all your time on you and your family, leaving no time for church or service to others

☐ Other:

Circle the habit you will immediately break in order to have a closer walk with God.

Is there really anything more important than getting closer to God? Now is the time to begin. Break the habits that hold you back. And make the decision, in God's strength, to start now.

1. Randy Pausch, "Really Achieving Your Childhood Dreams" (lecture, Carnegie Mellon University, Pittsburgh, PA, 18 September 2007).

Alignment

■ Day 4 Aligning with Your Goals

You have examined clarity and movement in your quest to have a closer relationship with God. Now you will look at the issue of alignment, making certain all you do moves you toward the accomplishment of your goals. We will suggest five ways you can align your life's activities with your mission statement.

■ Looking in the Mirror: Honest Self-Assessment

The simple life means we have to face the reality of who we are. It means facing some potentially tough issues.

In our research we asked whether respondents were good spiritual leaders in their families. Only 22 percent strongly agreed they are good spiritual leaders. Nearly half, 46 percent, only somewhat agreed. The remaining 32 percent admitted they are not good spiritual leaders. It's the "somewhat agree" group that got our attention.

Why would nearly half of those surveyed respond with uncertainty about such an important issue? It would seem many in this group were just not being completely honest with themselves. They were hopeful but not realistic.

simplelife   STATISTICS ■

22% *strongly agree they are good spiritual leaders.*
46% *somewhat agree they are good spiritual leaders.*
32% *say they are not good spiritual leaders.*

For example, we asked Karl, a software developer in a suburb of Kansas City, why he could not answer the question with greater certainty.

"Well," he began hesitatingly, "I think I do a pretty good job of being a spiritual leader in my family. And I'm known at work as a guy who doesn't cuss or drink. I pray sometimes, so I guess I can't be all that bad as a spiritual leader."

When we asked Karl whether his wife and children would describe him as a spiritual leader, he curtly responded, "I'm not sure what they would say."

"Are you a regular Bible reader?"

"Who is?" he questioned in response.

"Do you regularly attend church?" His curious response to that question was "I don't know."

We didn't need to spend much time with Karl to see that he really didn't have an honest self-assessment of his relationship with God. To remedy this problem, Karl could take a discipleship inventory like the one in *MasterLife* or the one in Brad Waggoner's book *The Shape of Faith to Come*. We encourage you to take such an inventory for a more objective view of your relationship with God.

If you don't want to take time for an inventory, answer these questions to evaluate your walk with God.

Am I closer to God today than I was a year ago?
☐ Yes   ☐ No
Is prayer a regular part of my day?
☐ Yes   ☐ No
Do I read the Bible at least two or three times a week?
☐ Yes   ☐ No
Am I truly connected to a local congregation?
☐ Yes   ☐ No
Do I freely talk with family and others about my faith?
☐ Yes   ☐ No

When we presented these questions to Karl, he was at first defensive. But after a few moments his tone changed. "Look," he began, "I guess I hadn't really been honest with myself. I'm not really walking with God. I have a long way to go. But I guess I need to start somewhere."

Karl was taking the first step toward alignment.

▪ Talking to Someone: Accountability

Let's suppose you included in your mission statement a desire to attend church regularly. What form of accountability works best for you?

Ella from Oregon responded without hesitation. "I just told my three kids we needed to start going to church," she said with a grin. "I'm a single mom with absolutely no time, so I've pushed God out of my life. But when I told the girls we were going to church, they started reminding me every Saturday night and waking me up on Sunday mornings. That was all the push I needed."

Indeed, many respondents in our study indicated they had accountability approaches. "I got involved in a Bible-study group at a church a few miles from me," Sandra told us. "The people in the group are great; but if I miss a study, they text-message me before the day is over." Others hold each other accountable by phone.

A few of the respondents were accountable to themselves. If such a statement sounds contradictory, that was our first reaction as well. But George from Texas disagreed. "I keep my relationship with God strong by writing in a journal," he said. "I write with total honesty. And I can tell if I am getting off track by what I write in my journal. And I know I'm really getting off track if I fail to write something in my journal every day."

On page 152 you identified someone with whom you would share your mission statement. Identify a way you would like this person to hold you accountable for keeping your actions aligned with your goals.

■ Recognizing Who You Are: The Personality Match

Countless self-assessment tools are on the market today to help us identify our strengths and weaknesses, our leadership style, our personality traits, and our spiritual gifts. But you don't have to take an inventory to know some things about yourself. You know what you like and what you don't like. And you know what works in your life and what doesn't. In fact, we found that many people are out of alignment in their relationships with God because they are trying to do something that goes against the grain of their personalities and the way God made them.

I (Thom) get bored and distracted easily, and I have learned that this personality trait affects my relationship with God. I have trouble focusing during prayer time. My mind often wanders. For years I felt guilty because I just didn't do well being quiet and still. Then I tried praying while I walked, and I learned I could focus much better while walking than in solitude in a room by myself. My personality is better suited for activity, even in prayer.

Many struggle in their relationships with God because they try to be someone else. God accepts us as we are. Listen to the comments of some of those who get this idea:

- "I read my Bible in 15-minute increments. It helps me better grasp the meaning than if I did one long reading."
- "My prayer time is the first thing in the morning before the kids get up. It's the only time I have alone, and it's my best time of day."
- "I started becoming more faithful in my church attendance when I began going to the early-morning service. That's just a better time of day for me."
- "I used to force evangelistic conversations on people, although it wasn't really my style. I stopped doing that and started praying that God would give me opportunities for natural conversations. It has been amazing! I am now sharing my faith more than ever."

The simple life requires alignment. And alignment means understanding who you are and playing to your strengths, personality, and gifts.

Write several words that describe the following.

Your personality:

Your gifts:

Your training and education:

Your skills and abilities:

Based on your unique personality and gifts, what alignment steps would enhance your walk with God?

■ Being Willing to Realign: Flexibility

"Sometimes," Michael told us, "I just wonder if I will ever get this right. Since I became a Christian more than 10 years ago, I have tried to have a closer walk with God. When I was single, I had no problem with time for prayer and studying God's Word. But now I am married with two preschool sons. I'm having a tough time doing things the way I used to."

Guess what, Michael? You probably can't do things the way you used to!

Michael has family responsibilities he didn't have a few years ago. He has time constraints that are different. He has to realign.

The apostle Paul was the master of realignment.

Read Acts 16:6-10. Identify three ways the Holy Spirit redirected Paul and his companions.

1.

2.

3.

Paul saw every closed door as an opportunity to find an open door. And he finally found his place of alignment with God's plan for him.

Alignment will probably lead to realignment. And realignment means you won't always get it right, but then you try again. Realignment may also mean you get it right for a while, but you have to adjust or change as God changes the circumstances of your life. Like Paul, stay sensitive to God's leadership and be obedient to His direction for the next step. He is drawing you into a deeper relationship with Himself.

As you have begun aligning your life with your mission statement, in what ways do you already need to realign?

How do you know you need to realign?

■ Accepting Your Humanity: A Willingness to Be Imperfect

If you have been a Christian for any length of time, you may have noticed that being a Christian doesn't mean you stay sin-free. Even Paul talked about his struggle with sin.

Read Romans 7:19,24-25. Describe Paul's dilemma.

In what areas of your life do you struggle with sin as Paul did?

Even though we have been saved by faith in Jesus, we still sin. And although our sin nature doesn't give us an excuse to sin, we have the promise of forgiveness. No matter how hard we try, we can never do everything perfectly.

Some fail to enter the simple life because they are perfectionists. If they don't do things exactly right, they consider themselves failures. Are we talking to you?

Meet Rebecca from Des Moines, Iowa. Rebecca is a perfectionist. And it is about to kill her. "My pastor told me I needed to have a one-hour quiet time every day," she said nervously. "I did fine the first three days; and then, boom, a dozen urgent matters got me off focus. The same thing has happened to me in my Bible-reading time. In fact, it seems like every time I try to do something right, I fail. I really wonder if it's worth the effort at all."

Although we should strive to draw closer to God, we also need to understand that amazing thing called grace. Because of what His Son did for us, God loves us unconditionally. We don't seek to please Him so that He will love us. We seek to please Him because we desire to respond to His grace and love.

If you are a perfectionist, relax in the simple life. Jesus said it best: "Come to Me, all of you who are weary and burdened, and I will give you rest" (Matt. 11:28). Shed the perfectionism and rest in Jesus.

If you are a perfectionist, identify ways your tendency is keeping you from aligning your actions with your goals for a closer walk with God. Ask God to help you rest in Him.

Focus

Jamie really didn't think she should be complaining. Basically happy, she said, "Most of the areas of my life are good. I have three good kids. My husband and I have a good relationship. And I guess I'm one of the few people out there who really like their jobs." Jamie hesitated. "But I know I'm not living for God. I'm not a big moral failure; it's just that I don't have a strong relationship with Him. God is just kind of in the background in my life."

We asked Jamie if she could elaborate.

"Before I had kids, I spent regular time in prayer. Now it seems that my prayer life is an occasional 'Help me, Lord.' I feel like I'm going through the motions at church. I have so many things on my mind that I find myself thinking about all the things I have to do."

"What would you like most if you could live a simple life?"

"Oh, that's an easy question. If I could really live a simple life, I would enjoy spending more time with God. Praying more. Reading the Bible more. Going on mission trips. Getting more involved in church. Getting into a women's Bible study."

So we asked the obvious question: "What's stopping you?"

"Let me see," she said, this time with a smile. "Three kids, ages 10, 12, and 15, who have to be transported a thousand different places. A job that requires more than 40 hours a week with commute time. A house that is never clean. Trying to keep up with some church activities. Helping the kids with their homework. Going to school functions."

So then we asked a leading question: "Is there anything you do that is more important than your relationship with God?"

She knew where we were headed.

"If you guys are trying to put me on a guilt trip, you're doing a good job," Jamie said sternly. "I know I need to give God more time. I just don't where to begin. I don't know what I would eliminate."

Jamie nailed it. She said precisely what we heard throughout this research process. Sixty-nine percent of the respondents wished they had more time for church and other spiritual matters. The simple life is elusive because elimination is too difficult for most people.

Do you struggle with eliminating activities from your life in order to have more time for God?   ☐ Yes   ☐ No

How can we begin to focus on things that really matter? How can we eliminate just a few items when they all appear to be necessities? Perhaps a journey back in time can give us some perspective.

■ The Not-So-Simple Life Two Thousand Years Ago

We have heard many churchgoers say they wish the church today could be just like the early church in the Book of Acts. But things were not always perfect in Jerusalem.

Read Acts 6:1-7. What was causing dissension in the church?

What did the apostles identify as their top priorities?

What solution was adopted to meet ministry needs?

Notice the incredible response in Acts 6:7 when the apostles remained focused:

1. The preaching ministry grew more powerful.
2. More people became followers of Christ.
3. Some of the hardest to reach became Christians.

The early church leaders' example provides us with five key principles that help us focus today.

Deal realistically with your messy world. How many times have we postponed the simple life because we were certain that, when life's circumstances change, we would have all the time in the world? "When I finish my education, then I can simplify my life." "When the kids are grown, I can have a normal life." "When this major crunch at work has passed, then I can do some things that really matter."

The early church leaders dealt with the messiness of life straight on. A significant group in the church was complaining. The gospel focus of the early church was in danger of being lost. The widows of Greek origin were being neglected in the church's provision of food.

The leaders didn't say they would forego matters of utmost importance to deal with the tyranny of the urgent. They didn't say they would ignore the matter either. They acknowledged the messiness of life and then dealt with it.

Be brutally honest with yourself and others. Look at Acts 6:2 closely: "The Twelve summoned the whole company of the disciples and said, 'It would not be right for us to give up preaching about God to wait on tables.' " Sometimes the first step is the toughest because it means we can't fool ourselves anymore. If God is in the background of our lives, it clearly means we have lost our focus on the simple life that really matters.

Notice that the apostles told everyone ("the whole company") about the challenge, making it clear they would lose focus on their main calling ("preaching about God") if they took a detour to get involved in yet another activity ("wait on tables").

Acknowledge that something good has to go. One of the most important ministries of the Jerusalem church was taking care of the widows. The biblical mandate to care for widows is evident throughout Scripture (see 1 Tim. 5:3; Jas. 1:27). But the leaders of the church couldn't do it all. They had to let something go, even if it was something good.

Be creative in discovering alternatives. Sometimes we are too busy, even too busy for God, because we have our own minimessianic complex. We just don't believe it will be done unless we do it ourselves. The leaders of the early church knew the ministry to widows was important. They just didn't believe everything depended on them.

So the apostles looked for an alternative plan that would let them continue to focus on their primary calling. They found seven others who were physically and spiritually qualified to carry out the task (see Acts 6:5).

Keep your focus. The temptation must have been great for the early church leaders to take on the task themselves. They must have felt pressure to abandon what really mattered to handle the most vocal issue of the moment. But they didn't. They kept their focus: "We will devote ourselves to prayer and to the preaching ministry" (Acts 6:4).

Focus. Not easy. But it's a must for the simple life.

Describe the way each principle applies to your personal need to focus on God.

Deal realistically with your messy world:

Be brutally honest with yourself and others:

Acknowledge that something has to go:

Be creative in discovering alternatives:

Keep your focus:

We can't escape the fact that nothing else really matters in life if our relationship with God isn't all it should be. If we are too busy for God, we are just too busy.

Many of us insist that everything we are doing, all of the activities we are involved in, and every minute that is consumed are nonnegotiable. We just can't eliminate anything.

Except time with God.

Elimination is a spiritual issue because it's a matter of stewardship. Eliminating the nonessentials, even if they are good things, is vital because God says it's important.

Paul wrote, "Pay careful attention, then, to how you walk—not as unwise people but as wise—making the most of the time, because the days are evil" (Eph. 5:15-16). The apostle Paul had two Greek words he could have used for *time* in this verse: *chronos* and *kairos*. *Chronos* refers to time in general. It is clock time and the root word for *chronological. Kairos* refers to a predetermined, specific amount of time. It is measured, allocated, and fixed.

Paul used *kairos.* His word choice is significant. He was saying, in essence, that you have a specific amount of time here in this world. That's it. It is already set. It is fixed. The clock is ticking. Your time is running out. Even now.

So make the most of it. Don't just spend it. Invest it. Be wise with the time God has given you. Eliminating activities, as God leads, is choosing to be a wise steward of the time and resources He has given. Elimination is vital to having focus. And focus is indispensable to the simple life and a closer relationship with God.

> Describe what your spiritual life would look like if you made the most of your time.

We heard several success stories from people who now spend more time with God because they have been successful at eliminating the extraneous. Here are a few.

- "I watched television an average of 15 hours a week. I made a commitment to cut my television time to 10 hours a week and gave the other 5 hours to prayer and Bible study. I now have about 45 minutes for prayer and Bible study each day that I didn't have before."
- "I spend 8 or 9 hours a week commuting to work. I decided to eliminate the time I listened to the car radio. Instead, I now listen to the Bible on CD and spend time in prayer. I also have a lot less road rage now!"

- "My ritual included reading the local paper for 45 minutes each morning. I limit myself to 30 minutes now and use the other 15 minutes each day for prayer."
- "It floored me when I decided to measure my time on the Internet for one week. Twenty hours! I couldn't believe it. I immediately cut that time in half and began studying books of the Bible."
- "I run about 45 minutes each day. I love listening to music and interesting speakers on my iPod. Now I listen to downloaded sermons and Bible readings at least three or four of the days I run each week."

What can you eliminate or reduce to make more time with God?

☐ TV	☐ E-mail	☐ Texting
☐ Movies	☐ Cell phone	☐ Magazines
☐ Computer	☐ Music	☐ Recreation
☐ Video games	☐ Leisure reading	
☐ Other:		

Write your commitment to devote more time to God. What will you eliminate? How much time will you try to gain each day or week? How will you spend your time with God?

The simple life may require some tough choices. It will probably require the elimination of something you are doing now. And it will mean saying no to things that threaten to pull you off track. But it will free you to do things that are really important—the things that really matter. That's the only way you can bring God from the background of your life to the foreground, the rightful place He deserves.

Evaluate your progress this week by answering these questions.

Clarity

Review your mission statement for your relationship with God (p. 151). Evaluate how you are doing. Do you need to make any adjustments?

Movement

Are you praying each day for God to give you strength to remove obstacles to your goals? Are you letting go of past failures and sins so that you can move forward?

Alignment

Does your mission statement fit your unique personality, gifts, and abilities? Do you need to make any adjustments to match your actions to the unique you?

Focus

Have you identified activities you need to eliminate that will allow you to have more time for God? Do you need to do anything else to get closer to God?

Look back over the past several days of moving closer to God. What lessons have you learned from Him during this time?

How to Put It All Together

SESSION 6
Group Experience

1. Share actions that can lead to a closer relationship with God.
2. Do you need to spend more time with God? Why or why not?
3. How can regular church attendance help you grow spiritually?
4. Is there a disconnect between your priorities and your practices when it comes to the Bible? Identify the areas of disconnect.
5. How comfortable are you discussing spiritual matters with others? How does openness about God affect your relationship with Him?

Clarity

1. Share your mission statements for a closer relationship with God.
2. Evaluate each mission statement by using these criteria:

   • Does it reflect a desire to grow closer to God?
   • Does it include an intentional plan for reaching goals?
   • Is it a realistic starting point?

Movement

1. Read Philippians 3:12-14. How did the apostle Paul move toward his spiritual goals?
2. Discuss ways a believer effectively leaves the past behind.
3. Read Philippians 4:6. What obstacles keep you from a deeper, more regular prayer life?
4. Examine your mission statement and indicate whether the steps you have outlined are incremental.
4. On what part of your mission statement do you tend to procrastinate? What part will you commit to implement immediately?
6. Share failures in your spiritual life that have tempted you to give up.

Alignment

1. What alignment is needed between your actions and goals?
2. Refer to page 166. Based on your personality and gifts, what alignment steps would enhance your walk with God?
3. How have you had to realign since you started working toward your mission statement?

Focus

1. What keeps you from staying focused on your relationship with God?
2. React to these five principles to stay focused on spiritual goals.

   - Deal realistically with your messy world.
   - Be brutally honest with yourself and others.
   - Acknowledge that something good has to go.
   - Be creative in discovering alternatives.
   - Keep your focus.

3. Read Ephesians 5:15-16. Describe what your spiritual life would look like if you made the most of your time.

Making Plans

1. Show the DVD for session 6.
2. Identify things you have committed to eliminate to make more time with God. How will you spend your time with Him? Pray in pairs about your plans to work toward your mission statement.

Although there are no more group sessions, complete week 6 devotionals and activities. They will provide a plan for putting together all you have learned and will help you identify your next step in pursuing the simple life.

If you missed this session, go to www.lifeway.com/downloads to download this or any other session of Simple Life.

Week 1 began with the frantic tale of a life out of control. Instead of living a life of purpose and intentionality, the person lived a life of stress and chaos. And at the end of the day, our hero fell into bed, hoping to remember to take out the garbage the next morning. Maybe you could relate.

That was six weeks ago. We trust that a lot has changed for you during this time. Maybe some of these statements capture the differences that have taken place in your life:

- I am moving from painful to purposeful living.
- I am focusing on what's important in life instead of being a victim of the urgent.
- I am making forward progress in meeting my life goals— goals that became buried over the years, goals I never thought I'd achieve.
- My life is more in line with what God wants me to do.
- Having learned that I really can be disciplined and stick to my mission statements only makes me want to achieve more. What's next?

That's what we're going to talk about this week. Getting a taste of the simple life is like eating one potato chip: it leaves you wanting more. This week we'll guide you through a process that will help you identify the next step you need to take, as well as a comprehensive plan for staying on the path to the simple life.

Clarity

■ **Day 1** Clarity Toward the Simple Life

You have now applied the concepts of simple life—clarity, movement, alignment, and focus—to four big areas of your life—time, relationships, money, and God. Let's stop a moment and reflect.

> List three ways you have made progress toward the simple life during the past six weeks.
>
> 1.
> 2.
> 3.
>
> Has one particular Bible verse helped you work toward the simple life over the past six weeks? If so, write the Scripture reference here and circle it in your Bible.
>
> Record a word that describes your out-of-control lifestyle at the beginning of this study:
>
> Record a word that describes where you are now on your journey to a simple life:
>
> Record a word that describes your next goal for the simple life:

If the simple life still appears a little complex at this point, it's probably because you are wondering how you will make so many changes at once. Actually, we never intended for you to focus on all four areas at the same time. As you approach the last week of this journey, select one or two of the four big areas you desire to simplify the most.

Identify the one or two areas—your highest priorities—you will focus on this week.

☐ Time   ☐ Relationships   ☐ Finances   ☐ God

For example, you may determine that your most immediate needs are in the areas of relationships and money. You want to be a better spouse, parent, friend, or coworker, so you resolve to compliment the person each day for the next week. You also decide to reduce your debt. You have a four-thousand-dollar credit-card balance with a high interest rate, and you want to pay it off as quickly as possible.

Let's say you estimate eliminating your credit-card debt will take 18 months. In addition to your regular payment, you will add one hundred dollars a month to reduce the debt faster. That means you will cut back on other expenses by one hundred dollars each month. You write a mission statement to reflect your two highest priorities:

I will reduce my expenses on food and clothes by one hundred dollars a month and apply the savings to my credit-card balance. In addition, I will be a better husband by intentionally complimenting my wife at least once each day for a week.

After one week you may want to continue implementing the second part of your mission statement, or you might want to do something else to improve your relationship.

Time for clarity. Write your simple-life mission statement here, setting goals for the one or two areas you have decided to target.

Movement

Now that you have written a mission statement for the most significant needs in your life, think about the barriers that prevent you from making progress toward your goals or congestion that hinders free movement toward the simple life.

Think about some things that threaten to hold you back.
For example:

Have you neglected prayer?	☐ Yes	☐ No
Your mission is truly impossible without God.		
Have you forgiven others you need to forgive?	☐ Yes	☐ No
Have you accepted forgiveness in your life?	☐ Yes	☐ No
Have you accepted past failure as final?	☐ Yes	☐ No
Are you willing to try again?	☐ Yes	☐ No

Look back at the mission statement you wrote in day 1 (p. 182). What might hinder you from accomplishing it? Identify three or four points of congestion you will seek to remove in God's power.

Read Moses' charge to Joshua in Deuteronomy 31:7-8.

"Moses then summoned Joshua and said to him in the sight of all Israel, 'Be strong and courageous, for you will go with this people into the land the LORD swore to give to their fathers. You will enable them to take possession of it. The LORD is the One who will go before you. He will be with you; He will not leave you or forsake you. Do not be afraid or discouraged.' "

How do these verses apply to your simple-life journey thus far?

Moses never got to enter the promised land, but Joshua did. Have you reached the simple life? Have you arrived at your destination? If not, what remains to be done?

Remember, when the people finally entered the land God had promised them, they didn't sit down and do nothing. They had work to do.

What do you most need to do to continue moving toward your goals for the simple life?

Alignment

Have you ever been driving down the road and seemed to be going against all the traffic? Everyone appeared to be headed in the opposite direction. That makes driving easy, but the same situation in life can make you uncomfortable at best and miserable at worst. Have you ever felt that you were going in a different direction from everyone else? Maybe you like soccer when everyone else likes football. Maybe you are a vegetarian in a meat-eating family. Maybe you are a morning person when everyone around you is a night owl.

Maybe the situation is more serious. You might be so preoccupied with accomplishing tasks that you have little focus on God when you should be praying. Your church insists you'd be great with preschoolers, but you know working with youth is your passion. Maybe you feel called to be a missionary in the business world, but everyone else says you ought to preach.

The purpose of alignment is to make certain your actions are in sync with the purpose you are trying to accomplish. If you are not doing what God created, gifted, and purposed you to be, your life will always feel out of alignment. Even if your car is sailing down the highway with no traffic jams to hinder you, you still won't enjoy the journey if the wheels are out of alignment. In seeking to align your life, remember that you must first align with God's purposes for you.

Read aloud Jeremiah 29:11, emphasizing the word *you*.

" 'I know the plans I have for you'—this is the LORD'S
   declaration—'plans for your welfare, not for disaster,
   to give you a future and a hope' " (Jer. 29:11).

Review the personal qualities you checked in the activity on page 48. Have you discovered anything new about yourself in this journey toward the simple life? List any additional strengths, talents, gifts, or passions you have discovered.

Thank God for the unique blend of gifts He has given you.

Review the mission statement you wrote in day 1 (p. 182). Do the actions you identified align with your gifts and strengths?
☐ Yes ☐ No

List habits or actions in your life that you need to align with the goals expressed in your mission statement. What do you most need to work on?

Describe a time when you found great joy in doing something God created you to do.

You experienced joy because your actions were aligned with God's call and purpose for you. If you don't have that sense of alignment now, ask God to continue to reveal His plans for you as you seek to live the simple life.

Focus

■ **Day 4** Focus for the Simple Life

This week you have pinpointed the one or two facets of your life that need the most work. In day 1 you wrote a mission statement for your next step toward the simple life. In day 2 you identified areas of your life that are hindering you from making progress toward your mission statement (movement). In day 3 you considered your uniqueness, your strengths, and your weaknesses and identified areas of needed alignment. Now it's time to focus.

In the Sermon on the Mount, Jesus taught that people should be truthful. He said, "Simply let your 'Yes' be 'Yes,' and your 'No,' 'No' " (Matt. 5:37, NIV). You've had to be honest with yourself throughout this study in order to align your daily actions with what you claimed to be the priorities for your life. You've had to say no to some things, even good things, that were part of your life just a few weeks ago, and you've had the opportunity to open doors and say yes to some priorities that had been crowded out in the past.

> Name three hard noes you've learned to say since beginning your simple-life action plan.
>
> 1.
> 2.
> 3.

Because you've said no, you may have been able to say yes to some things for the first time in a long time. For example, one woman dreamed of being a concert pianist, but marriage and children buried that goal. She rightly gave her attention to her husband and kids;

but when the last child left for college, she began her piano lessons again and practiced for hours a day. The dream was still alive. She said yes to it because she was at a stage in life when she could responsibly say no to other things.

Because you have said no, how have you been able to say yes? Name three yeses you have affirmed during this study.

1.
2.
3.

How have these yeses helped you stay focused on your goals?

Read the mission statement you wrote in day 1 (p. 182). Identify anything—even something good—you need to cut out of your life to focus on your goals.

How does this decision enable you to move toward your goals?

simple life

We began this book by articulating the quest for the simple life. According to our surveys and research, people needed help in four major areas: time, relationships, money, and God. The vast majority of the respondents clearly told us that the first of the big four had to be God.

In week 5 we took you through a simple process for getting closer to God in the simple life. Remember, if you are missing out on close fellowship with God, nothing else matters. God longs for a deeper relationship with us. That's the foundation on which everything else is built. The simple life will simply not work without God. Make sure you are gaining ground in this all-important area of life.

> Is anything keeping you from making progress in your relationship with God? Review your responses to the activities in week 5 as you answer the following questions.

> **Clarity**
> Examine your mission statement for a closer relationship with God (p. 151). Does it accurately express your goals for your relationship with God? Spend time in prayer seeking God's heart. Be sure your statement is specific and measurable. Make any revisions here.

Movement
Are there still obstacles that are blocking your relationship
with God?   ☐ Yes   ☐ No

If so, identify them and ask God to help you remove them.

Alignment
Are your daily actions aligned with your goal
of getting closer to God?   ☐ Yes   ☐ No

Focus
Have you cleared out the clutter—even good things—
to have time for God?   ☐ Yes   ☐ No

Ask God to show you adjustments you need to make to draw
closer to Him. Then record any commitments you wish to make.

You've now completed this study, but you are never completely finished with this process. After you have simplified your life in the one or two areas you identified in day 1 (p. 182), follow the same process to tackle one or two other areas of your life that need attention.

Thank you for going on this journey with us. We have both prayed for you, even though we don't know you by name. Our prayer has been that God would use this study to move His people to be more like Him in all we are, all we say, and all we do. And that is our prayer for you. "I pray this: that your love will keep on growing in knowledge and every kind of discernment, so that you can determine what really matters and can be pure and blameless in the day of Christ, filled with the fruit of righteousness that comes through Jesus Christ, to the glory and praise of God" (Phil. 1:9-11).

Two Ways to Earn Credit
for Studying LifeWay Christian Resources Material

Christian Growth Study Plan resources are available for course credit for personal growth and church leadership training.

Courses are designed as plans for personal spiritual growth and for training current and future church leaders. To receive credit, complete the book, material, or activity. Respond to the learning activities or attend group sessions, when applicable, and show your work to your pastor, staff member, or church leader. Then go to *www.lifeway.com/CGSP*, or call the toll-free number for instructions for receiving credit and your certificate of completion.

For information about studies in the Christian Growth Study Plan, refer to the current catalog online at the CGSP Web address. This program and certificate are free LifeWay services to you.

CONTACT INFORMATION:
Christian Growth Study Plan
One LifeWay Plaza, MSN 117
Nashville, TN 37234
CGSP info line 1-800-968-5519
www.lifeway.com/CGSP
To order resources 1-800-458-2772

Need a CEU?

Receive Continuing Education Units (CEUs) when you complete group Bible studies by your favorite LifeWay authors.

Some studies are approved by the Association of Christian Schools International (ACSI) for CEU credits. Do you need to renew your Christian school teaching certificate? Gather a group of teachers or neighbors and complete one of the approved studies. Then go to *www.lifeway.com/CEU* to submit a request form or to find a list of ACSI-approved LifeWay studies and conferences. Book studies must be completed in a group setting. Online courses approved for ACSI credit are also noted on the course list. The administrative cost of each CEU certificate is only $10 per course.

CONTACT INFORMATION:
CEU Coordinator
One LifeWay Plaza, MSN 150
Nashville, TN 37234
Info line 1-800-968-5519
www.lifeway.com/CEU

Life a blur?

TIME
RELATIONSHIPS
MONEY
GOD

simple life

THOM S. RAINER & ART RAINER

Here's some focus.

Simple Life breaks it down
into four key sections:
TIME, RELATIONSHIPS,
MONEY & GOD
and by applying four key goals:
CLARITY, MOVEMENT,
ALIGNMENT & FOCUS
you can foster a more
joyful and less busy life.

B&H
BOOKS

Available at LifeWay Christian Stores | ChurchLeadershipBooks.com